PUB WALKS

The Kennet

Canal

TWENTY CIRCULAR WALKS

Nigel Vile

COUNTRYSIDE BOOKS
NEWBURY, BERKSHIRE

First published 1997
© Nigel Vile 1997

Revised and updated 2002

All rights reserved.
No reproduction permitted without the prior
permission of the publisher:

COUNTRYSIDE BOOKS
3 Catherine Road
Newbury, Berkshire

To view our complete range of books,
please visit us at
www.countrysidebooks.co.uk

ISBN 1 85306 453 X

Designed by Graham Whiteman
Cover illustration by Colin Doggett
Photographs and maps by the author

Produced through MRM Associates Ltd., Reading
Printed by Woolnough Bookbinding Ltd., Irthlingborough

Contents

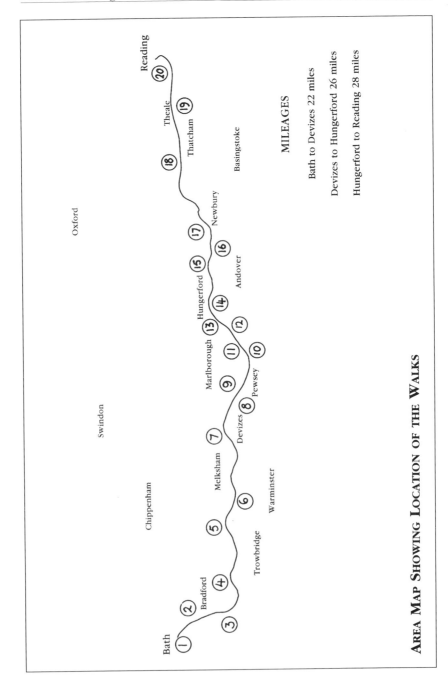

AREA MAP SHOWING LOCATION OF THE WALKS

MILEAGES

Bath to Devizes 22 miles

Devizes to Hungerford 26 miles

Hungerford to Reading 28 miles

Walk

PUBLISHER'S NOTE

We hope that you obtain considerable enjoyment from this book; great care has been taken in its preparation. However, changes of landlord and actual closures are sadly not uncommon. Likewise, although at the time of publication all routes followed public rights of way or permitted paths, diversion orders can be made and permissions withdrawn.

We cannot of course be held responsible for such diversion orders and any inaccuracies in the text which result from these or any other changes to the routes nor any damage which might result from walkers trespassing on private property. We are anxious though that all details covering the walks and the pubs are kept up to date and would therefore welcome information from readers which would be relevant to future editions.

Introduction

(k̲ₐ̲) This book is part of a series entitled *Pub Walks Along ...* which builds on the success of the existing *Pub Walks* series by using middle and long-distance paths as a basis for circular pub walks. In addition to acting as a guide to pubs along the way, each book provides an ideal introduction to the long-distance path by incorporating sections of it into circular walks that are full of interest and yet generally undemanding. In this particular case, each walk explores a section of the Kennet and Avon Canal, together with a slice of the surrounding countryside through which this magnificent waterway passes.

The origins of the Kennet and Avon can be traced back to the 18th century. A simple advertisement in a Salisbury journal in 1792, announcing a meeting in Devizes to discuss a proposed waterway to Bristol, caused businessmen from that city to head into the depths of the Wiltshire countryside. An infamous 'Ride to Devizes' ensued, that was immortalised by at least two local poets of the time! There was clearly no shortage of venture capital, attracted by the high returns earned on such investments elsewhere in Britain. A line was surveyed by the engineer John Rennie, Royal Assent was granted in 1794, and in the same year work began on the Kennet and Avon Canal.

The river Kennet between Newbury and Reading had been navigable since the early 18th century, as had the Avon Navigation between Bath and Bristol. All that remained was to bridge the gap between Bath and Newbury, a mere 57 miles, and London would have a direct link with Bristol. With the exception of the 16 locks that make up the Caen Hill flight at Devizes, the Kennet and Avon was completed by 1807. Temporarily, a tramway lifted the barges up this famous incline. By 1810, work on Caen Hill was completed and the *Bath Herald* was able to report that 'the guns were fired on Sydney Wharf' alongside the canal's headquarters in Cleveland House.

Life on the canal followed an all too familiar pattern. There was an initial boom – the canal carried 341,878 tons of freight in 1838, for example. The main cargo was coal, moved to the Kennet and Avon by means of the Somerset Coal Canal from Radstock and Paulton. There followed inevitable competition from the railways, with the Great Western Railway opening its line between London and Bristol in 1841. Canal tolls were slashed and redundancies were declared, the losses mounted up and eventually the Kennet and Avon was sold to the GWR for a princely £210,415! The canal was deliberately run down and neglected so that by 1955 the Rusholme survey listed it as grade III – 'canals which are either disused or carry insufficient trade to justify their retention as commercial waterways.'

In the post-war years, the Kennet & Avon Canal Trust has worked closely with the British Waterways Board to breathe fresh life into this great waterway. Lock gates have been replaced, lock chambers re-bricked, leaking canal beds lined with concrete and any number of YTS trainees have been equipped with basic manual skills while undertaking restoration work. All this sweat and toil was rewarded in August 1990 when the Queen journeyed west to Devizes to officially reopen the Kennet and Avon Canal. Forty years of dedication and hard work have produced a national asset that will undoubtedly attract thousands of visitors to the canal, a veritable jewel in the BWB's vast network of inland waterways.

This book combines information on the whole length of the Kennet and Avon – including possible accommodation for long-distance walkers – with detailed descriptions of 20 pubs and circular walks at various points along the towpath. Pubs which have been selected are as close to the canal as possible – in some cases literally alongside the towpath. As such, they range from freehouses and pubs owned by small independent brewers, through to inns owned by the large national brewery chains.

For each pub, a pen portrait has been included. This covers its history, its character, the food on offer and the range of beers and ales available. Clearly, the information is only accurate at a point in time, but it is more than adequate to give the reader an overall feel and impression of the pub.

Generally speaking, most pubs should be open at lunchtimes between 11.30 am and 2.30 pm, with food being available between 12 noon and 2 pm. Equally, in the evenings you can expect the opening hours to extend from 6 pm to 10.30 pm, with food available from around 7 pm. However, pub opening hours are the subject of constant change and variation, depending upon demand, seasonal factors and occasionally the whim of the landlord. Therefore, rather than specify opening hours in each case, only to be proven wrong by the time the book goes to print, each pub's telephone number is included should you wish to make a precise enquiry. Most pubs display their opening hours at their main entrance, enabling this information to be obtained before you set off on your walk.

The walks are generally of modest length, making them suitable for all kinds of walkers from the more mature person to the typical family group. Each should provide a morning or an afternoon of exercise and interest, which can be followed by a relaxing meal and a drink in the relevant pub. Whilst the directions and sketch maps in the book are adequate for route-finding – compasses won't be needed in this part of the world! – it is better for the walker to back this up with an OS map. The appropriate OS Landranger sheet, 1:50 000, is specified for each walk, and should be as much a part of your equipment as the obligatory waterproof clothing and stout footwear.

Parking should be done with due consideration. If you intend to visit the pub following the walk, then it is only common courtesy to seek the landlord's permission prior to leaving your vehicle in his empty car park in the morning. On most occasions, landlords are only too happy to oblige. If you are doing a walk and not visiting the pub, then you have no right to use the patrons' car park. Whatever the circumstances, in nearly every case I have indicated alternative parking arrangements in the vicinity of each pub.

At the end of your walk, you could well be hot and sticky, damp and muddy. It is only polite therefore to both the landlord and his other customers if you attempt some form of wash and brush-up after your walk. If nothing else, at least leave muddy walking boots in your car.

I hope that this book will bring you many hours of pleasure. Not only do these walks open up one of Britain's premier waterways, they also introduce some excellent canalside inns and public houses. I wish you many happy hours of walking.

Nigel A. Vile

BATHAMPTON
The George
❧❦❧

The gentle canal section of this walk follows a stiff climb onto the hills surrounding Bath by way of Widcombe Hill, from whose slopes visitors can enjoy perhaps the best view of the city. The climb to the 'skyline of Bath' is hard work, but the rewards make every bead of perspiration worthwhile!

Bathonians have for many years enjoyed this inn's fine location alongside the towpath of the Kennet & Avon Canal. Although the sign on the wall dates the current building as c1840, the history books tell a far different story. Here was once a hostelry for the ancient priory of Hampton, with origins that could go back as far as the 14th century. Intriguingly, underground passages are thought to link the inn with the neighbouring church and vicarage. In the late 18th century, Viscount du Barry, victim of the last legal duel fought in Britain, was laid out for his wake in one of the inn's lounges, before his burial in the nearby churchyard.

Internally, the George is an interesting collection of stone, low-ceilinged rooms, with beams, horse brasses, old rifles, oil paintings and sherry barrels. The atmosphere is decidely traditional. It is the food, however, for which the George has earned an enviable reputation. There is an extensive menu, which includes vegetarian dishes as well as a number of specials, with such tempting choices as pork in blackberry and orange, chicken Stroganoff, salmon and asparagus quiche, and chicken and broccoli bake on offer. This is in addition to the staple fare of pubs – salads, ploughman's and sandwiches. The sweets are equally inviting and include chocolate fudge pudding, Caribbean pancake, and pineapple and custard flan. Thirsts can be quenched with one of a number of fine beers, including Courage Best and Directors, Bass and Irish Beamish, whilst a good selection of wines is listed on the wine menu.

The George is very popular, with its canalside location and delightful garden attracting large numbers of walkers, cyclists, bargees and motorists. Being so close to the City of Bath, it is equally popular as a lunchtime watering hole with the local business community. A relaxed and friendly ambience is the order of the day at this fine old inn, crowds or no crowds. Telephone 01225 425079.

● **HOW TO GET THERE:** Leave Bath on the A36 Warminister Road. Less than 2 miles out from the city centre, an unclassified road on the left-hand side – Bathampton Lane – leads down to Bathampton village. Follow this road through the village, and across the Kennet & Avon Canal, and the George is on the left-hand side.

● **PARKING:** There is a large car park for patrons to the rear of the George. There is also plenty of room for roadside parking in Tyning Road, adjacent to the inn and alongside the canal.

● **LENGTH OF THE WALK:** 6 miles. Map: OS Landranger 172 Bristol and Bath (inn GR 776665).

THE WALK

Cross the canal using the canal bridge, continue along Bathampton's High Street for 300 yards and turn left into Down Lane. Follow Down Lane uphill to the A36 and cross the main road with care, before following the enclosed bridlepath opposite that climbs towards

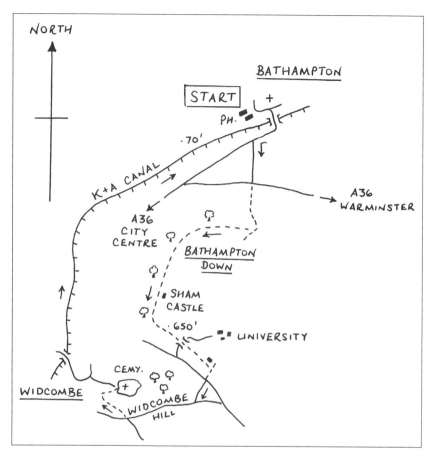

Bathampton Down. The path reaches a gate in 250 yards. Continue on the bridlepath ahead, as it winds its way to the hilltop.

Almost at the hilltop, the path bears to the right. In a short distance, where the path heads up towards the golf course, bear right to follow the edge of the hilltop. Continue ahead towards an area of woodland, a short distance to the right of a pair of masts. Continue across the edge of the hilltop to a stile, immediately above the tree line. Beyond the stile, follow the right-hand edge of Bathampton Down for ½ mile until you reach Bath Golf Course clubhouse. Pass to the right of the buildings, through the car park and onto the enclosure containing Sham Castle.

Bathampton Down was once the site of extensive stone quarrying. Sham Castle, perhaps the best known of England's 18th-century follies, was built for Ralph Allen, the architect of Georgian Bath, as an eye-catcher to enhance the view from his house in the town centre.

Pass into the adjoining field via a stile, and follow the right-hand edge of this field for 400 yards until you come to the second stone slab stile. Cross the stile, cross the wooden footbridge across Quarry Road and continue ahead along the right-hand edge of a sports field belonging to Bath University. This path shortly reaches the University's Computer Services Department, where a gated lane in the right-hand corner of the car park is followed down to the main road.

Cross over into Copseland, which runs through to Widcombe Hill. Follow the pavement downhill for almost ½ mile, until you reach the junction with Prospect Road on the left. This section of road walking soon brings far-ranging views across the City of Bath. Cross the stile on the right, signposted as the Bath Skyline Walk. Drop down to a gate on the left, pass through the gate and bear half-right across a hillside field. Drop down towards Bath, keeping a line with the abbey, to the bottom corner of the field and a stile. Once past this stile, turn sharp right and follow a fieldpath down towards a cemetery nestling in the shadow of Smallcombe Wood. Aim for a stile in the bottom corner of the field.

 Once across the stile, turn left to follow Horseshoe Road down towards Bath. The road shortly reaches Horseshoe Walk, where you turn left and follow the pavement for 300 yards to the canal. Cross the waterway, before following the towpath to the right for 2½ miles. Beyond the locks, the canal passes through Sydney Gardens, constructed in 1795. The K&ACC paid 2,000 guineas for the right of passage through the gardens, and the canal architecture had to match the ambience of the surrounding landscape. This necessitated decorative tunnel entrances and ornate footbridges. Along the way, the path changes banks at Bathwick Hill and again immediately before Sydney House, before you find yourself back at the George.

K_A KENNET & AVON CANAL

Walks 1 and 2 connect at the George Inn at Bathampton.

Walk 1 joins the canal 300 yards from the point where it leaves the river Avon. The 'missing' section of towpath passes Bath Deep Lock and Thimble Mill, where steam pumps once pumped water from the Avon to the top of the Bath flight of locks.

BATHAMPTON
The George
❦

The Kennet & Avon towpath between Bathampton and Claverton is an absolute delight, with steep woodland tumbling down the hillsides either side of the canal. Adjectives like 'sylvan' and 'resplendent' spring readily to mind. It is not difficult to appreciate why this area is one of the most popular walking destinations around the Bath and Bristol region. Away from the towpath, the walk passes through Claverton village before climbing high onto Bathampton Down.

This attractive creeper-covered canalside pub is also the starting point for Walk 1. Full details of the George appear in Walk 1, together with information on how to get there and where to park.

- **LENGTH OF THE WALK:** 5 miles. Map: OS Landranger 172 Bristol and Bath (inn GR 776665).

THE WALK

(K) From the George, follow the towpath to the south, away from Bath, for 2 miles until you reach Claverton. Early in the walk, Hampton Wharf marks the point where a tramroad running from Bathampton Down joined the canal. Wagon loads of stone from the hilltop quarries were carried by barge into Bath and used in the construction of many of the city's finest buildings. Further on, the canal passes above the historic pumping station in Claverton. Water was raised from the Avon into the canal by channelling the river's power against two coupled waterwheels which worked a pair of beam engines. Designed by the canal's engineer, John Rennie, the pumping station has been restored and is open to the public on Sunday afternoons in the summer.

Leave the towpath at the overbridge in Claverton – number 180 – and follow the lane uphill towards the A36 and Claverton village. In just 50 yards, where the lane bears left, climb some steps and cross a stile on the right. In the field beyond, bear left up to a kissing gate and a path that leads up to the A36. Cross the main road with care, before following a path alongside a bus shelter up to the main street in Claverton.

In St Mary's church, you will find a quite magnificent mausoleum that marks the earthly resting spot of Ralph Allen, one of the founding fathers of Georgian Bath. Above St Mary's, high on Bathampton Down, the walk later passes by a number of overgrown rock faces, the site of extensive quarrying that provided so much of Ralph Allen's building material.

Follow the road to the left through the village to a road junction, where you turn right and climb steeply up the hillside for 1/2 mile to the entrance to the American Museum. This is housed in the former Claverton Manor, an English neo-classical mansion designed in 1820 by Sir Jeffry Wyatville. A series of furnished rooms brings to life the history of the American people. The museum is open every afternoon (excluding Monday) from the end of March to the end of October. Two hundred yards past its entrance, climb some stone steps in the wall on the right to a signposted fieldpath.

Follow this path to the right of Bath University's firing range, and onto a stone slab stile that marks the entrance to the NT's Bushey Norwood property. Beyond the stile, turn sharp right and follow the field boundary to the corner of the field, where you turn left to continue along the edge of this large hilltop enclosure. In 1/2 mile, in

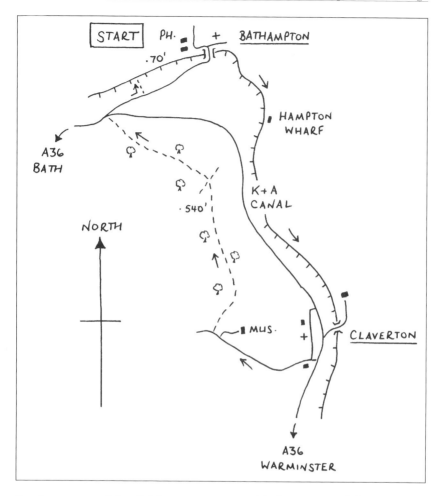

the far corner of the field, you come to a kissing-gate and the entrance to Bathampton Wood.

Follow the path directly ahead through the woodland, an area of former quarrying activity, for ¼ mile to a prominent crosstrack. This was the tramline that descended the hillside to Hampton Wharf. Do not follow this track, rather cross the iron stile opposite and continue following a woodland path that emerges onto the open hilltop of Bathampton Down in 300 yards. Cross the Down, keeping just above the bushes on the right so as to enjoy the views across the Avon valley.

In 300 yards you reach a wall and a stile, beyond which the path continues across Bathampton Down. Do not cross this stile, but follow

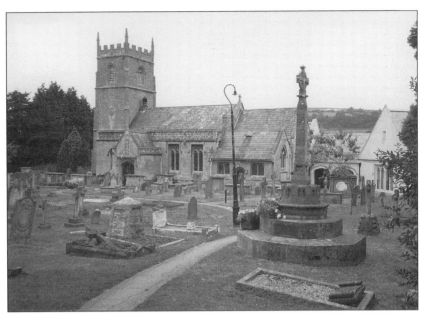

St Nicholas church, Bathampton.

the path downhill on the right that shortly becomes an unmetalled track that descends steeply to reach the A36 in $^1/_4$ mile. Cross the main road with extreme care, before following Bathampton Lane to the right. In 150 yards, turn left down a side turn signposted to Meadow Croft and Meadow View.

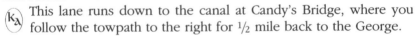 This lane runs down to the canal at Candy's Bridge, where you follow the towpath to the right for $^1/_2$ mile back to the George.

 KENNET & AVON CANAL – CLAVERTON (OVERBRIDGE 180) TO DUNDAS WHARF ($1^1/_4$ MILES)

The towpath sticks to the eastern side of the canal through to Dundas, where a footbridge is crossed and the path switches to the western side of the waterway. This section of the canal is dominated by the magnificent natural landscape of the Avon valley, with steep wooded slopes tumbling down to the river.

WALK 3
AVONCLIFF
The Cross Guns

East of Bath, the Kennet & Avon Canal passes through the Limpley Stoke valley. With its steep wooded slopes and breathtaking vistas, this is without a shadow of doubt the most magnificent natural landscape along the whole length of the canal. Away from the canal towpath, the walk begins by climbing the valley's hillsides to explore a slice of the West Wiltshire countryside. As well as far ranging views and the village of Winsley, with picturesque St Nicholas' church, the walk passes through Conkwell Wood.

Avoncliff is a remote hamlet, deep in the Avon valley between Bath and Bradford-on-Avon. A pair of flock mills on the river gave rise to the settlement, but it was the coming of the Kennet & Avon Canal in the late 18th century that most influenced life in the valley. The Cross Guns dates back to the 17th century, and was therefore frequented by the local weavers long before it became a bargees' watering hole.The inn enjoys a most attractive location, sandwiched between the canal and

17

the river Avon. The terraced gardens at the front of the Cross Guns provide excellent views of both the river and the magnificent aqueduct. The Cross Guns is a marvellously old fashioned pub, with a vast stone fireplace, stone walls, low beams and solid oak tables. The increasing popularity of the inn with walkers, cyclists and canal-users does mean that the small bar area can become very crowded. However, there are a large number of picnic tables on the terraces, where food and drink can be enjoyed overlooking the river.

The Cross Guns has developed something of a reputation for the quality and value of its food. Naturally, the standard pub fare of sandwiches and ploughman's is on offer, but beyond this are a number of other most appetising dishes. These could include home-made steak and kidney pie, perhaps preceded by some home-made pâté, a variety of steak dishes and a number of fish options. These typically include lemon sole, trout and crab. The Cross Guns is a freehouse, and offers as a consequence an interesting range of beers and ales. These could include Smiles BB, Ruddles BB and Tanglefoot, as well as Ushers BB and Courage Best.

With its superb location, its traditional interior, the good selection of beers and the fascinating canal architecture, the Cross Guns is a truly excellent pub to visit. It justifiably earns an entry in most good pub guides. Telephone: 01225 862335.

- **HOW TO GET THERE:** Not easy! As the A363 climbs Masons Lane out of the centre of Bradford-on-Avon, there is a sharp right-hand bend. Turn left at this point into Newtown, along a road signposted to Turleigh. In 1 mile, a left-turn is signposted to Avoncliff. This cul-de-sac lane leads to a small parking area in Avoncliff, alongside the Kennet & Avon Canal. From this parking area, it is a short walk across Avoncliff Aqueduct to the Cross Guns.
- **PARKING:** There is no car park at this remote inn. See above for details of local parking facilities, but with these being inadequate at peak times, you may wish to start this walk at Dundas, with its large lay-by alongside the A36 Warminster Road, and visit the Cross Guns en route.
- **LENGTH OF THE WALK:** 5 miles. Maps: OS Landrangers 172 Bristol and Bath and 173 Swindon and Devizes are both needed for this walk (inn GR 805600).

THE WALK

Follow the signposted footpath out of the parking area, away from the canal, up a flight of steps and into a hillside pasture. Climb to the top right-hand corner of this field, where you reach a track leading from

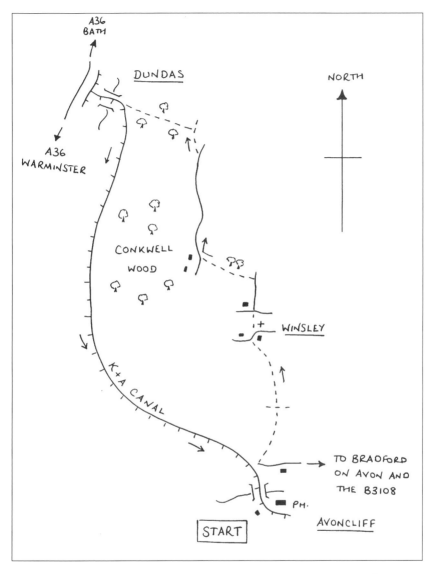

Turleigh down to the canal. The views from this point across the Avon valley towards Westwood on the opposite hilltop are worth pausing to enjoy. Cross this track, pass through the kissing gate opposite and continue along an enclosed footpath which climbs the hillside towards Winsley. At the top of the hill, the path joins a quiet lane which is followed through to the B3108 in the centre of Winsley, the lane

Dundas Wharf.

bearing left by the village bowling club before joining the main road.

Turn right, and follow the B3108 past the Seven Stars pub to a sharp right bend. At this point, turn left along the road leading to St Nicholas' church. Just past the church, turn right to follow a path alongside the churchyard which brings you into Millbourne Close. Turn left and, at the next junction, follow Late Broads to the right to reach the Winsley by-pass. Follow the lane opposite, beside Church Farm, which is signposted to Conkwell.

In 200 yards, pass through a gateway on the left into a field and follow the left-hand field boundary across towards a small copse. Cross the stile to the left of this copse, and head directly across the next large field to a stile beneath a prominent tree. This stile bring you onto a quiet lane beside Conkwell Grange Farm. Follow the lane to the right for ¹/₂ mile until, just beyond a residence called Coptoak, you bear left onto a footpath leading into Conkwell Wood. A rather delapidated footpath sign bears the legend 'Dundas'.

(K) In 200 yards, follow the track on the left which leads downhill to join the canal towpath at the eastern end of Dundas Aqueduct. This was once the trackbed of a quarry tramline carrying limestone from the quarries around Conkwell to the canal. Follow the towpath across the aqueduct to reach Dundas Basin. Just past the basin, cross a footbridge on the left to the far side of the canal. Follow the canal past the crane alongside the basin, across the entrance to the Somerset Coal Canal and across the opposite side of Dundas Aqueduct, with its doric columns standing proudly alongside Dundas Wharf. The wharf marks the junction with the Somerset Coal Canal, whose black gold was more than anything else responsible for the commercial success of the Kennet & Avon in its heyday.

Continue along the towpath through the Avon valley for 2½ miles back to Avoncliff. Less spectacular than its neighbour, Avoncliff Aqueduct is nevertheless a fine monument to John Rennie, the canal's engineer. Beneath its vast central arch, the Avon formerly powered a pair of flock mills; one is now a handsome residence, the other sits in genteel decay. You are now soon back at the Cross Guns.

 KENNET & AVON CANAL

Walks 3 and 4 connect at Avoncliff.

BRADFORD-ON-AVON
The Canal Tavern

*This delightful excursion follows both the river Avon and the Kennet &
Avon Canal between Bradford-on-Avon, once described as a miniature
Bath, and neighbouring Avoncliff, which is of particular interest for its
industrial past. The return along the canal follows an elevated course
above the river. This watery paradise has been designated the Barton Farm
Country Park, where you may see moorhens, coot, mallard, heron and the
occasional kingfisher.*

The Canal Tavern, constructed of the local freestone, backs onto the
Kennet & Avon immediately below Bradford Lock. The origins of the
pub are rooted firmly in the waterway with some of its earliest licensees
– the Edmunds family – also being boatbuilders on the adjoining Lower
Wharf. It was at this spot, too, that the first sod was cut in the

construction of the canal in October 1794.

Inside the Canal Tavern, there are two adjoining bars at the front, a dining room at the rear and an attractive courtyard that sits literally alongside the towpath. The bar areas are fitted out with both wooden flooring and carpets, with some wood panelled walls and traditional beams. The bars are furnished with darkwood tables and chairs, and the occasional settle, whilst various items of canal memorabilia decorate the walls. These include prints and photographs of the waterway, one or two canal signs and various pots and churns painted in the traditional bargees' fashion. The overall effect is a traditional and welcoming pub, where both locals and visitors feel very much at home.

A wide range of food is available at the Canal Tavern, with the bar menu covering starters, vegetarian dishes, jacket potatoes, baguettes, main meals, children's dishes and a range of desserts. Daily specials are also chalked up in the bar. Amongst the more tempting dishes on offer are steak and ale pie, smoked chicken and bacon tagliatelli, risotto, jacket potatoes filled with cheese, ham and onion, and baguettes filled with prawn, apple and celery.

The Canal Tavern is a Wadworth hostelry, with fine beers such as Henry's IPA and the ever popular 6X usually available. The brewery also produces seasonal beers, which means that Old Timer might be available during the winter months, and Summersault in the summer, fine beers which can be enjoyed in a delightful canalside setting. Telephone: 01225 867426.

- **HOW TO GET THERE:** Follow the B3109 Frome Road from Bradford-on-Avon's town centre for just $1/4$ mile, and the Canal Tavern lies on the right-hand side immediately before the Kennet & Avon.
- **PARKING:** There is restricted roadside parking on the Frome Road opposite the Canal Tavern. No restrictions apply on Sundays. An alternative is to park in the station car park in Bradford, just a short distance from the pub.
- **LENGTH OF THE WALK:** 3 miles. Map: OS Landranger 173 Swindon and Devizes (inn GR 825603).

THE WALK

Follow the Frome Road back towards Bradford's town centre before taking the first turning on the left into Pound Lane. (If you have parked in the station car park, follow the Frome Road out of town and it is first right into Pound Lane). Where the lane bears left into a car park, keep directly ahead and walk past Barton Farm and down to the river Avon

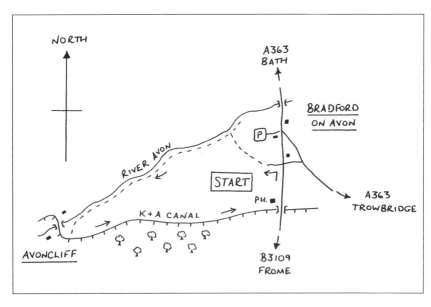

by an ancient packhorse bridge. Turn left, and follow the tarmac path beside the river for 1/2 mile to a point where the path climbs a slope away from the Avon up to the canal.

Turn right off the tarmac path at this point to follow a footpath that continues alongside the river. This path passes to the right of a sewage works, before crossing a stile into a riverside meadow. Follow the riverside path across several fields for close on 1 mile until you reach the weir in Avoncliff. At this point, turn left to reach some wooden steps in the corner of the field.

Climb these steps to reach the towpath. A detour to the right will enable you to explore Avoncliff, with its aqueduct, Canal Bookshop, Cross Guns Inn and tearooms. The settlement was founded on local stone and woollen industries, with a pair of flock mills being located on the river just upstream of Avoncliff Aqueduct. The main walk follows the towpath to the left for 1½ miles back to Bradford. In Bradford, the canal passes the town's lock and wharves. The lower wharf was sited alongside the Canal Tavern, with the upper wharf still very much in evidence above Bradford Lock. Here we find a dry dock, a wharfinger's house and a Canal Trust shop, as well as countless moored vessels that combine to produce an idyllic canalside scene. The path passes Bradford's well known tithe barn before reaching the Canal Tavern.

The lock-up and Town Bridge.

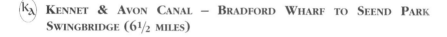

KENNET & AVON CANAL – BRADFORD WHARF TO SEEND PARK SWINGBRIDGE ($6^1/_2$ MILES)

The towpath follows the northern bank of the canal all the way between Bradford Wharf and Seend Park Swingbridge on walk 5. Features to look out for along the towpath include Biss Aqueduct on the edge of Trowbridge, Semington Aqueduct, and the site of the junction with the Wilts and Berks Canal in Semington alongside locks 15 and 16.

WALK 5

SEEND CLEEVE

The Barge Inn

Hereabouts, the canal borders the southern boundary of the North Wiltshire Clay Vale, and the limestone hills around Bath and Dundas are but a distant memory. It is almost as if the Kennet & Avon Canal is pausing for breath before the rigours of the Caen Hill Locks just a few miles distant. The villages of Seend and Seend Cleeve, midway between Trowbridge and Devizes, straddle a small ridge of hills overlooking this section of the canal. Along the waterway lies a selection of locks and an old iron works site.

It might be just 5 miles along the Kennet & Avon Canal from Seend Cleeve to Devizes, but the short haul includes a staggering 30 locks. The Barge Inn must have come as something of a blessing to the bargees, a welcome source of sustenance before the rigours of the next few miles. The inn stands on the site of the former Seend Wharf, where as well as ale for the barge-owners, there was stabling and rest for the hauliers' horses.

The Barge is a fine old inn, only recently modernised to make the most of its magnificent waterside location. Crafted of local Bathstone, and with a fine garden overlooking the Kennet & Avon, it is not difficult to see why the Barge has become one of the area's most popular hostelries. Victorian gas lamps line the water's edge, whilst hanging baskets, flower tubs and ivy adorn the inn and its environs.

Internally, the Barge is comfortably decorated with oak tables and chairs, whilst milk churns serve as bar stools. Finely painted flowers with a Victorian feel decorate both the walls and ceiling, a horticultural theme that is continued with the bunches of dried flowers that decorate the bar area. On those cold winter evenings, the original fireplace with its black-leaded grate will provide welcome warmth.

The range of food available at the Barge has earned it a well-deserved reputation. Snacks might include jacket potatoes, home-made soup, ploughman's, chicken and mushroom pie or scampi, whilst youngsters can choose from their own reasonably-priced selection of dishes. The dining area overlooking the canal provides customers with a more extensive menu that changes every few weeks. Traditional appetites might enjoy a rack of lamb or sirloin steak, while wild mushrooms with green beans, butterbeans, broccoli and sliced almonds in a provençal sauce will interest more sophisticated palates. The Barge is a Wadworth house, which makes the renowned 6X beer almost obligatory. This famous local brewery has been producing fine ales from its Devizes headquarters since 1885. Telephone: 01380 828230.

- **HOW TO GET THERE:** 2 miles east of Melksham on the A365 Devizes road, turn south onto an unclassified road signposted to Seend. In just under ½ mile, turn right again along a lane signposted to Seend Cleeve. In a short distance, just after the lane crosses the Kennet & Avon Canal, you will find the Barge Inn on the right-hand side.
- **PARKING:** There is a car park for patrons behind the Barge, and room for roadside parking in the vicinity of the inn.
- **LENGTH OF THE WALK:** 3½ miles. Map: OS Landranger 173 Swindon and Devizes (inn GR 932613).

THE WALK

Leave the Barge car park and turn right, following the lane into Seend

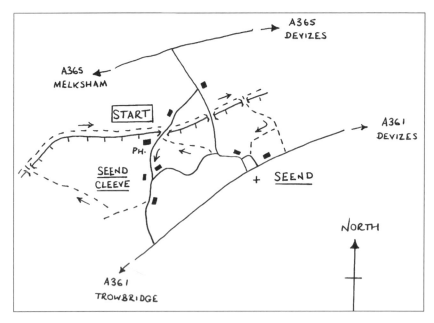

Cleeve. In ½ mile, just before Rew Farm on the left, turn right into Park Lane. Beyond a cottage, Park Lane continues as an unmetalled bridlepath for 150 yards to a pair of gates. Turn sharp right, and follow the right-hand hedgerow across the next couple of fields. Beyond a gate in the corner of the second field, continue directly ahead across a couple of smaller fields to Seend Park Swingbridge and the Kennet & Avon Canal.

Follow the towpath to the right for 1½ miles until you reach the swingbridge beyond Seend Top Lock, number 21. This is Rusty Lane Swingbridge. Along this section of the towpath, you will pass the five locks that make up the Seend Flight, the Barge Inn and the site of Seend Iron Works beside lock 19.

Cross the swingbridge, and follow an enclosed track for ¼ mile to the hilltop above the canal. At the top of the climb, turn right at a junction of paths to follow an enclosed track along the edge of the hilltop. This path brings fine views across the clay vale towards Melksham and beyond. In 250 yards, the path bears left away from the hillside and continues to a road leading to a small housing development. Turn right at this road, continue the short distance to a road junction and turn right again. In 300 yards, where the main road bears right downhill towards the Melksham to Devizes road, continue

28

The canal at Seend.

ahead along the lane signposted to Seend Cleeve.

In just a few yards, cross a stile on the right to follow a signposted footpath across an open field. The path passes to the right of a fine beech copse, before bearing left to head downhill towards the canal. Cross a stile in the fence ahead, before dropping down to lock 19. The bumpy ground beside this lock is all that remains of the Great Western Iron Ore Smelting Company, which in the mid 19th century extracted and processed the local ore deposits. Just past lock 19, a stile brings you onto the road beside the adjoining overbridge. The Barge Inn lies just to your left.

KENNET & AVON CANAL – RUSTY LANE SWINGBRIDGE TO FOXHANGERS LOCKS (2 MILES)

The towpath continues following the northern bank of the canal, with the sites of Scott's and Wragg's Wharves in Seend and the diminutive Summerham Aqueduct being passed along the way.

DEVIZES
The Black Horse

The magnificent flight of locks known as the Caen Hill Staircase, is the climax of this walk, which initially explores the countryside to the north of the canal. Along the way lies the village of Rowde, in the shadow of Roundway Hill, whose magnificent chalk escarpment dominates the view during the early stages of the walk.

The Kennet & Avon Canal has to climb 237 feet from the Avon valley into the centre of Devizes, necessitating 29 locks in just 2 miles and the centre-piece of this flight of locks is the Caen Hill Staircase, 16 consecutive locks that form one of the great wonders of the British canal network. Alongside each lock is a pound, a side reservoir to replenish the water lost each time a narrow boat passes through the flight, and these have become havens for wildfowl, including coot, moorhen, mallard, mute swans and heron. Just above the top lock, the canal passes beneath the busy Bath Road before reaching the Black Horse. Sandwiched between the main road and the waterway, this red-brick hostelry is part of the Wadworth estate. The rather inauspicious roadside outlook contrasts markedly with the inn's rear garden, with its picnic tables directly alongside the waterway.

Customers walk into a small bar area, with a flight of stairs giving access to a comfortable lounge bar that overlooks the canal. The bar areas are carpeted throughout, and are furnished with pine table and chair sets and cushioned settles. China plates, plants, old beer bottles and pots are displayed on shelves around the bar, whilst prints, photographs and maps decorate the walls of the Black Horse. The Kennet & Avon Canal features strongly in these pictures, with particular emphasis on the Caen Hill Staircase.

As well as the regular bar menu, which focuses on the standard pub fare of grills, steaks, fish dishes and poultry, the day's specials are displayed on blackboards in the bar area. Specials might typically include deep-fried breaded brie, sweet and sour chicken, swordfish steak in lemon sauce, trout stuffed with prawns and vegetable lasagne. Lighter snacks include a range of rolls and sandwiches, soup, and sausage in French bread. Desserts include apple pie and mince pie.

Wadworth brews such as 6X and Henry's Original IPA are available at the Black Horse, together with bottled Old Timer. This classic ale, normally available between October and March, is a rich copper-brown beer with a strong fruity, malty aroma. The Caen Hill Staircase, a canalside pub and traditional Wiltshire ales – the perfect combination! Telephone: 01380 723930.

- **HOW TO GET THERE:** The Black Horse fronts onto the main A361 Bath Road on the western outskirts of Devizes. Just before the Bath Road crosses the canal, you will see the red-brick hostelry on the left-hand side.
- **PARKING:** There is a car park for patrons alongside the Black Horse. There is also unrestricted roadside parking in the vicinity of the inn, albeit on a rather busy main road.
- **LENGTH OF THE WALK:** 4 miles. Map: OS Landranger 173 Swindon and Devizes (inn GR 001618).

THE WALK

From the Black Horse, immediately before the bridge across the canal, follow the drive on the right signposted to the Waterway Manager's Office. This lane runs alongside the canal to a BWB compound. Follow

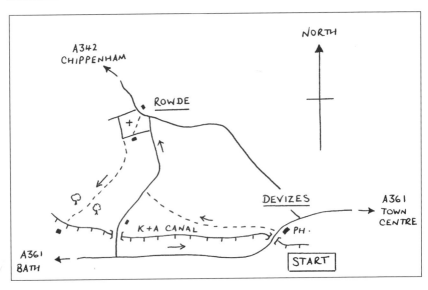

the track to the right of the compound, until it ends at a group of farm buildings bearing the legend 'No entry – farm only'. The footpath passes to the left of the farm buildings to emerge onto a gravelled track. Take this track down across the open countryside for ½ mile until you join the B3101, the views to the north being dominated by Roundway Hill. A copse of beechwood crowns the hilltop, where the Battle of Roundway Down was fought in July 1643.

Turn right, and follow this occasionally busy route into Rowde. The grass verge reaches to the village, where you follow the pavement down to the A342 alongside the Cross Keys Inn. As you enter the village, you will see 19th century Rowde Court on the left-hand side.

Turn left along the A342 for a short distance until, just before the George and Dragon Inn, you follow a lane on the left signposted 'To the Church and the Old Vicarage'. St Matthew's church was originally established in the 12th century, although the tower, nave and aisle are of more recent origin. Follow the path across the churchyard, on through a metal handgate and down a tarmac path into a housing estate. Turn right along Rowde Court Road and, in 150 yards, where the road bears right to head back to the A342, turn left along a pot-holed lane leading out of the village. This lane, which eventually becomes a secluded bridlepath, is followed southwards for ¾ mile towards the canal. It eventually reaches a stile and an open field.

Cross the stile, turn right and follow the right-hand hedgerow to the

Caen Hill Locks.

bottom corner of the field. Cross a pair of stiles in the corner of the field, alongside a pond, to reach the canal and Foxhangers Locks. To your left, a path leads to lock number 24. Cross the footbridge over the canal by lock 24, and follow the towpath to the left for 1½ miles back up the A361 Bath Road. This section of the walk takes you the whole length of the Caen Hill Staircase. Leave the canal at the Bath Road, turn left and the Black Horse is just a few yards along the A361

 KENNET & AVON CANAL – THE BLACK HORSE TO HORTON (3½ MILES)

The towpath follows the southern bank of the canal for all but the ¼ mile between the Town Bridge and the Wharf in Devizes. The respective crossover points are well signposted. The main feature along this section of the waterway is Devizes Wharf, where you will find the Canal Trust Offices and Information Centre.

HORTON
The Bridge Inn
❦

East of Devizes, the Kennet & Avon Canal follows a meandering course across the flat and fertile Vale of Pewsey. This walk passes a small area of upland called the Knoll, with the spectacular North Wessex Downs forming a magnificent backdrop. Beneath the hills lies Bishops Cannings, a village dominated by the 30 foot spire of the church of St Mary the Virgin, a replica in miniature of Salisbury Cathedral.

The Bridge Inn stands by a typical Kennet & Avon brick overbridge, from which it takes its name. Prior to becoming a licensed hostelry in 1810, the inn was a terrace of two houses together with a bakery and a mill. With the coming of the canal, the road had to be raised to pass over the bridge. As a result, the original ground floor was now below ground level necessitating the addition of a new top storey to retain the original height. Today's whitewashed building, with its hanging baskets and canalside garden, is deservedly a popular hostelry with both canal-users and locals.

Internally, the Bridge consists of a number of interconnected bar areas that lead out to the attractive garden. The decor, a mixture of wood-panelled walls, dark red paintwork, brick and beams, lends the inn a relaxed and comfortable feel, complemented by polished pine tables and chairs, the occasional settle and a large open fireplace. Around the walls are displayed a number of interesting photographs and prints, including several old shots of the canal.

The bar menu is displayed on a series of blackboards beside the bar. Dishes might typically include ham off the bone, smoked mackerel, home-made pâté, salmon steaks, vegetable quiche and deep fried cod. A selection of ploughman's meals is also available, together with a range of delicious baguettes. The fillings include fried steak and onions, grilled bacon and avocado and grilled cheese and tuna. During the summer months, a barbecue appears regularly in the garden, with its own menu. To complement your meal, there is an extensive wine list as well as a number of traditional beers served from the wood. These include Wadworth 6X and IPA, as well as Tanglefoot.

In recent years, the Bridge Inn has been totally refurbished. The decor and menu will be unrecognisable if you have not visited the hostelry for some time. The unpretentious inn of yesteryear, where local farming folk would stand over a pint, is rapidly earning a wide reputation for the quality and standard of its cuisine. You will find fine food and good beers at the end of a pleasant stroll through the Vale of Pewsey. Telephone: 01380 860273.

● **HOW TO GET THERE:** Follow the A361 Swindon road out of Devizes. About 2 miles from the town centre, on the edge of town, leave the main road at a roundabout to follow an unclassified road on the right to Horton. In just over 1 mile, you will find the Bridge Inn at Horton on the right-hand side.

● **PARKING:** There is parking for patrons beside the Bridge Inn. For non-patrons, there is a small parking space on the left of the road, just by the inn.

● **LENGTH OF THE WALK:** 6 miles. Map: OS Landranger 173 Swindon and Devizes (inn GR 039632).

THE WALK

Cross Horton Bridge, and follow the canal northwards – or to the left! In a little over 1 mile, the towpath passes beneath Horton Chain Bridge. Continue along the canal for $1^1/_4$ miles, passing beneath

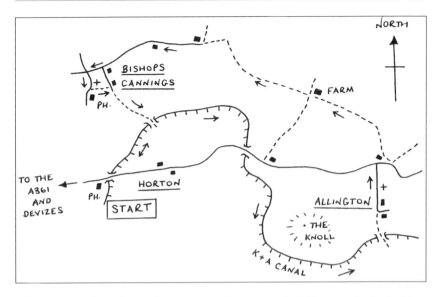

Allington Bridge along the way, until you reach Allington Swingbridge – number 129 – just to the south of Allington.

To continue on the pub walk, cross the bridge, and follow an enclosed track away from the canal into Allington. On reaching a lane, continue directly ahead for ¼ mile to the Devizes to Pewsey road. Turn right and, in 200 yards, a pair of bridlepaths are signposted on the left. Ignore the main track that heads northwards towards the North Wessex Downs. Instead, follow the narrow enclosed path on the left. This path runs behind a house, before continuing for ¼ mile to reach an open field. (NB. If this narrow path is heavily overgrown, it may be necessary to follow the edge of the field alongside the path. A gate on the left, a short distance along the main track mentioned earlier, gives access to the field in question.) Follow the field boundary directly ahead for ½ mile until you reach the complex of sheds and barns described on the OS map as Harepath Farm.

Just past these buildings, cross the drive leading to the farm and follow the enclosed bridlepath opposite that heads eastwards towards Bishops Cannings. The enclosed track shortly continues as an open path running across the top of a field. In the far corner of a second, smaller field, the path passes through a handgate on the right. Continue following the field boundary eastwards until, just below Easton Hill, the path drops down to a track which bears sharp left down to Easton Farm.

Boating through the Vale of Pewsey.

By the farm, the track forms a junction with a second track. Bear right, pass in front of a pair of red-brick cottages and follow a quiet lane for ³/₄ mile into Bishops Cannings. Continue on to a crossroads, 100 yards beyond the village primary school. Turn left and, in 150 yards, turn left into the village churchyard. Walk past the church and continue along Church Walk to a road junction. Turn right and, in 75 yards, continue ahead through a gateway to follow a private road – footpath only.

 In less than ¹/₂ mile, the path crosses the Kennet & Avon via a swingbridge. Follow the towpath to the right back to Horton Bridge, and the Bridge Inn.

 KENNET & AVON CANAL

Walks 7 and 8 connect at Allington Swingbridge.

HONEYSTREET
The Barge Inn
◄◙►

*B*etween *All Cannings and Honeystreet, the Kennet & Avon Canal continues its meandering course across the Vale of Pewsey. This is a rich agricultural landscape, set against the wonderful backdrop of the North Wessex Downs. Away from the towpath, this walk follows quiet byways and tracks across the Vale. The mysterious* Hanging Stone *lies in a field beside the bridlepath running between Hurst's Farm and Mill Farm, whilst the village pond in All Cannings lays claim to being the source of the Wiltshire* Moonraker *legend.*

The small settlement of Honeystreet originated around the Kennet & Avon Canal, with the waterway being responsible for bringing work to the area in the form of boatbuilding and a timber-yard. The proprietor of the timber-yard was responsible for the construction of the Barge Inn in 1858, the hostelry being erected for both his employees and passing bargees. In those days, the inn served as far more than a simple ale-house, being also a brewhouse, bakehouse, slaughterhouse, grocery shop and stabling facility. Its importance to the local community can be seen in the speed with which it was rebuilt following a fire in 1858. A plaque at the inn reads: 'Burnt December 12 1858. Rebuilt in Six Months by Samuel Robbins.'

Today the Barge remains an attractive stone inn that sits literally alongside the canal towpath. From the picnic tables outside the hostelry, there are fine views across the waterway towards the North Wessex Downs. Internally, there is one main bar, a smaller dining area and a games room. The bar offers customers a welcoming open fire, around which are gathered a number of comfortable armchairs. Around the rest of the bar are a good number of tables and chairs, together with pew seats and bar stools. Photographs of the Kennet & Avon hang around the walls of the inn, with the canal theme reinforced by a number of hand-painted canal artefacts.

Visitors will find a wide range of dishes available at the Barge, with the menu offering starters, grills, fish dishes, vegetarian dishes, lighter snacks, children's dishes and desserts. The day's specials are displayed on a board in the bar, and might typically include home-made vegetable soup, vegetable samosas, smoked mackerel, home-made cottage pie and cheesy pizza. The desserts will certainly have the waist-band expanding, with selections such as treacle sponge pudding, spotted dick and apple crumble being available.

The canalside tables offer a fine spot to enjoy a quiet pint on a warm summer's day. Being an Usher's house, the brews available include Ushers BB, Founders and Triple Crown. One customer found the beers so palatable that he recorded his achievements on a window in the bar: 'Sid Biggs got drunk, May 2nd 1872'. Tempting though it may be to emulate Sid Biggs, don't forget that you will in all probability have a car journey home! Telephone: 01672 851705.

- **HOW TO GET THERE:** Follow the unclassified road that runs eastwards from Devizes to Pewsey. Then, 6 miles east of Devizes, in the village of Alton Barnes, turn right along the road signposted to Woodborough. In ¹/₂ mile, having crossed the Kennet & Avon Canal, the Barge Inn is signposted along a cul-de-sac lane on the right.
- **PARKING:** There is a large car park for patrons by the Barge Inn. There is also room for roadside parking in Alton Barnes, alongside the village store. This is just a few minutes' walk from the canal.

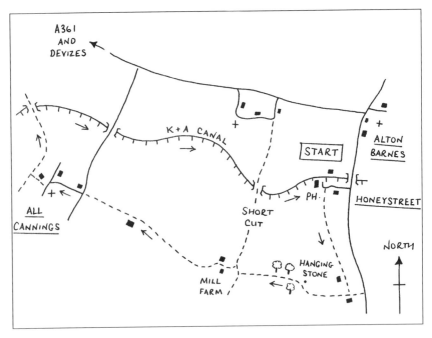

● **LENGTH OF THE WALK:** 6½ miles. Map: OS Landranger 173 Swindon and Devizes (inn GR 101615).

THE WALK

At the southern end of the pub car park, where the lane bears left to head into Honeystreet, cross a stile to follow the signposted footpath directly ahead into an adjoining field. Continue ahead alongside the field boundary to the corner of the field, where you pass through a gateway on the right. Immediately on your left is another stile, beyond which the fence on the left is followed across a larger field to a gate in the far left-hand corner. Cross the farm track beyond this gate, pass through the gateway opposite and continue across the next field to its left-hand corner. In the corner of the field, you pick up an enclosed track which is followed due south for ¼ mile to a junction with Hurst Lane, crossing one stile and passing Hurst's Farm along the way.

Follow Hurst Lane, an unmetalled bridlepath, to the right. In ½ mile, where the lane bears right and left in quick succession, the boulder in the field on the right is shown as 'Hanging Stone' on the OS maps. In another ½ mile, at a junction, turn right. In just 100 yards, bear left along the drive leading to Mill Farm. (NB. For a shorter walk, ignore the left turn to Mill Farm – continue north along the lane for 1/2 mile to Stanton Bridge and the Kennet & Avon Canal.) Follow the drive right up to the farmhouse. Just as you enter the farmyard by the house, follow the path on the left that runs between two farm buildings. Cross through a pair of gates, and follow a short section of enclosed path beside a stream. The path soon bears right, crossing another stream, before running to a handgate and an open field.

Follow the right-hand field boundary for 70 yards to a second handgate. In the next field, follow the left-hand field boundary for 500 yards until you come to a handgate in the hedge on the left. Beyond this gate, follow a concrete path to the right for 3/4 mile to a road junction on the edge of All Cannings. To the right, the North Wessex Downs rise impressively above the Vale of Pewsey. At the junction, follow the road opposite – signposted to All Cannings.

The village has a pleasing mixture of buildings, including many timber-framed and thatched cottages. All Saints' church contains a pair of ceiling-high memorials, one of 1587 with sculptured eagles and heraldic carvings to William Ernle of Etchilhampton, and a less ornate one to Sir John Ernle and his family from the 1730s. Just south of the church lies Manor Farm and the pond which is the alleged home of the *Moonraker* legend.

In 400 yards, just past the village green, bear left along the lane leading to the church. Opposite the entrance to the church, follow a signposted footpath on the right. This gravelled path soon becomes unmetalled and runs down to an open field. Cross a stile, and follow the field boundary to the right for 1/2 mile.

(KA) In the corner of the field, a path leads up to Allington Swingbridge and the canal. Follow the towpath to the right for over 2 miles back to Honeystreet. Along the way, you will pass Woodway Bridge, All Cannings Bridge, England's Bridge and Stanton Bridge. Honeystreet was a product of the canal, and it was from the local wharf that the last canal-based traders plied their craft. Robbins, Lane and Pinnegar were the descendants of what was originally Robbins & Co. Over the years, the company engaged in boat-building, as well as running a fleet of barges that brought in timber from Avonmouth and Hungerford. Whilst the wharf is now silent, a working timber-yard still trades beside the canal, heavy lorries bringing the timber onto the site. Other than that, this is a quiet section of the canal passing through the picturesque Vale of Pewsey, bringing you back to the Barge Inn.

Honeystreet moorings.

 KENNET & AVON CANAL – THE BARGE INN TO LADIES BRIDGE (2 MILES)

These 2 miles, with the towpath following the southern bank of the canal, are dominated by the fine natural landscape of the Vale of Pewsey, with Woodborough Hill and Picked Hill being particular landmarks.

WILCOT
The Golden Swan

❦

The Kennet & Avon Canal at Wilcot was cut through the grounds of Wilcot Manor, at the time the home of Lady Wroughton. As well as exploring this unique stretch of the waterway, the towpath borders Stowell Park. An unusual suspension bridge crosses the canal east of Wilcot, linking up areas of the Park that were served by the Kennet & Avon. Away from the canal, the walk begins by passing Holy Cross church in Wilcot and the neighbouring manor.

Those publicans whose hostelries can lay claim to a ghost certainly enjoy a head start in the marketing stakes! The fortunate licensee at the Golden Swan can go one better, with two spirits said to stalk the neighbourhood at certain times during the year. Ghost number one is that of a young girl who was cast out of the local vicarage one wintry Christmas Eve, her husband convinced that she was engaged in some sort of illicit affair with a village lad. She walked past the village inn before turning into the adjoining lane, where she was found dead the following morning – minus her right hand! If you visit the Golden Swan on 24th December, be warned . . . the so-called Grey Lady is known to retrace her fateful steps during the hours of darkness leading up to Christmas Day. A second local apparition is that of a coach and horses that has been seen rattling along nearby Hare Street. One imaginative theory is that the carriage driver is in search of the original Swan Inn, built in 1700 but destroyed by fire in 1859.

The Golden Swan itself is a most attractive, steeply thatched pub, surrounded by a good number of thatched cottages and dwellings that front onto Wilcot's village green. Inside the pub are two small bar rooms, both unpretentious and welcoming, each with beams and china displays. At the end of a midsummer walk, however, most visitors will prefer to relax on the inn's pretty front lawn, where a good number of rustic tables are provided for visitors.

The Golden Swan has earned a deserved reputation for its excellent home-cooked food. In addition to the traditional pub fare, a good selection of children's dishes and vegetarian meals are available. The portions also represent good value-for-money. Being a Wadworth pub, the Devizes-based brewer's IPA or 6X should be the natural brew to accompany your meal. Visit the Golden Swan in winter, and you may be fortunate enough to find a pint of Old Timer available. Old Timer – ABV 5.8% – is a rich, copper-brown beer with a strong fruity, malty aroma. Although only available between October and March, it is well worth seeking out a brew which the *Good Beer Guide* describes as 'a classic beer'. Telephone: 01672 562289.

- **HOW TO GET THERE:** An unclassified road runs across the Vale of Pewsey from Devizes to Pewsey. Wilcot lies on this road, 2 miles north-west of Pewsey. The Golden Swan lies in the centre of the village, 1/4 mile south of the Kennet & Avon Canal.
- **PARKING:** There is a small car park for patrons alongside the Golden Swan. There is also ample room for roadside parking in the vicinity of the pub.
- **LENGTH OF THE WALK:** 3 miles. Map: OS Landranger 173 Swindon and Devizes (inn GR 143611).

THE WALK

Turn left along the lane outside the Golden Swan, following the byway signposted to 'Wilcot Church Only'. In a little over 1/4 mile, just as you

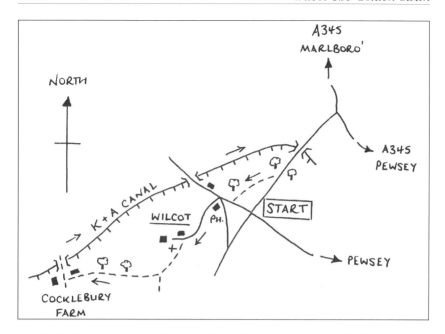

reach Holy Cross church, bear left along the unmetalled track that borders the southern edge of the churchyard. The church was rebuilt following a fire in 1737, with the manor dating from the 17th century. In 300 yards, turn right at a junction and follow a green lane for ½ mile to Cocklebury Farm.

Just past a group of farm cottages, turn right at a junction and follow a gated path to Ladies Bridge and the Kennet & Avon. The far side of the bridge gives access to the towpath, with Picked Hill being a prominent landmark just to the north of the waterway.

Lady Wroughton would only permit the navigation to pass through the estate if the waterway were carefully landscaped. The result was Wilcot Water and Ladies Bridge. Wilcot Water resembles an ornamental lake, whilst ornate façades and balustraded parapets ensure that Ladies Bridge appeased Lady Wroughton's aesthetic sensibilities.

Follow the towpath to the right, passing Wilcot Water, before reaching the overbridge in Wilcot. Continue along the towpath, passing beneath the unusual suspension bridge that gives access to Stowell Park. In another 600 yards, leave the canal at Bristow Bridge – which carries the numberplate 115.

Follow the lane to the right for 250 yards, to a gateway on the right in a small dip. Although this is an unclassified road, it is used as an

Ladies Bridge.

unofficial Pewsey by-pass. Take care – traffic can be surprisingly busy!
Pass through this gateway and cross the field beyond, following the
line of the left-hand field boundary. In 350 yards, cross a stile in this
field boundary. Follow the right-hand edge of the next field, alongside
an area of woodland, to a gate that gives access onto the Pewsey to
Wilcot lane. Turn right at the road, and in just 150 yards you will find
yourself outside the Golden Swan.

 KENNET & AVON CANAL

Walks 9 and 10 connect at Bristow Bridge

PEWSEY WHARF
The French Horn

At Pewsey, the Kennet & Avon Canal is nearing the end of the 15-mile Long Pound between Devizes and Wootton Rivers. The waterway edges its way gently along the eastern edges of the Vale of Pewsey, almost in preparation for the final climb to the summit at Crofton. To the south, the canal borders the infant river Avon. The wet meadow and scrub alongside the river is a nature reserve, with one access point being off the towpath just east of Pain's Bridge. North of the canal, the walk climbs Oare Hill.

Pewsey Wharf lies ½ mile north of Pewsey, the 'capital' of the Vale of Pewsey. The settlement around the wharf was entirely the result of the navigation being cut through the Wiltshire countryside some 200 years ago. The navvies who worked on the Kennet & Avon are often depicted as a hard-drinking, no-nonsense group of individuals, probably of Irish stock! On this section of the canal, however, local tradition maintains that French prisoners of war provided the manpower. At the end of each day's labours, they were summoned back to their prison by the sound of a horn . . . hence the unusual name for this canalside hostelry.

The French Horn is constructed of red brick, in keeping with so many other buildings in the Vale of Pewsey. Internally, there is a comfortable lounge bar and an adjoining dining area. Brickwork, wood-panelling, pine beams and white paintwork give the bar areas a bright and fresh feel, with dried flowers, pots, prints and a former inn sign adding complementary touches to the decor. With a mixture of darkwood and pine table and chair sets, together with log fires, the French Horn offers a warm welcome to its visitors.

The day's menu appears on blackboards inside the lounge bar. A good selection of home-made dishes is always available – wholesome portions of well-prepared and imaginative food. Typical selections might include snacks such as jacket potatoes, baguettes and soup, whilst more substantial dishes include blue cheese lasagne, fisherman's pie, steak and ale pie, liver and bacon and steak and kidney pie. The baguettes offer good value-for-money, and include fillings such as hot pork, spicy sausage, bacon and tuna mayonnaise. The soup of the day on a recent visit was spicy parsnip. All of the main dishes are served with a pot of fresh vegetables. An equally appealing range of desserts is available, that might include kiwi fruit cheesecake, banoffi pie, apple crumble and chocolate bread and butter cream pudding.

The French Horn is a Wadworth hostelry, and naturally serves the Devizes-based brewery's flagship ale, 6X. A lesser known beer is Henry's Original IPA, which the *Good Beer Guide* describes as 'a golden-brown coloured beer with a gentle, malty and slightly hoppy aroma.' Two fine Wiltshire beers, which could be enjoyed in the French Horn's rear garden following a delightful excursion in the Vale of Pewsey. Telephone: 01672 562443.

- **HOW TO GET THERE:** Pewsey Wharf is 1/2 mile north of Pewsey on the A345 Marlborough road. The French Horn lies just to the north of the canal, alongside the main road.
- **PARKING:** There is a car park for patrons to the rear of the French Horn. To the south of the canal, at the Wharf Centre, there is parking for visitors to the canal.
- **LENGTH OF THE WALK:** 6 miles (or 5 miles if the short loop at the beginning is omitted). Map: OS Landranger 173 Swindon and Devizes (inn GR 155612).

THE WALK

Follow the lane alongside the French Horn. Beyond a gate, continue through an enclosure that lies just above the Kennet & Avon. At the far side of this enclosure, the path passes through a gateway to enter an area of recently planted woodland. Follow the path through this plantation for just 600 yards, until you emerge onto the lane leading from Oare to Wilcot.

(k) Turn left and cross Bristow Bridge, before turning left to follow the towpath in an easterly direction. In ¹/₂ mile, you will pass Pewsey Wharf.

The small settlement at Pewsey Wharf, the pub, a warehouse and a few canalside cottages, lies just to the north of the town itself. The Kennet & Avon was essentially a rural canal, and this would have been an outlet for the produce of the Vale of Pewsey, as well as the source of Pewsey's coal supplies. Pewsey can also claim to be the place where the idea for an annual canal race to Westminster was originated. In 1948, a local gentleman offered £20 to anyone who could go by boat from Pewsey to Westminster in 100 hours.

In ¹/₂ mile you pass Pain's Bridge and in another mile you reach Milkhouse Water Bridge. Between Pain's and Milkhouse Water Bridges, you will pass one of the entrances to the nature reserve that lies alongside the river Avon. At the access point, a map is displayed that details the permissive paths criss-crossing this delightful habitat. A detour into the reserve is highly recommended, although the going is extremely boggy underfoot.

To continue the pub walk, leave the canal at Milkhouse Water Bridge, and follow the lane over the canal and northwards towards the Downs. In ¹/₂ mile, the lane passes between a pair of stone gateposts alongside some cottages. Continue along the lane towards the hills until, beyond the left turn to West Wick House, the lane becomes an unmetalled path. Continue along this path, still heading towards the Downs. The path reaches a gate at the foot of the hills, beyond which the path forks. Bear left, and climb steeply up the hillside. At the top of the climb, pass through another gateway. After 20 yards, bear left through another gateway and continue along the path ahead to the trig point that marks the summit of Oare Hill.

On the summit of the hill lies the Giant's Grave, an ancient burial chamber that is now marked by a pair of humps on the ground. Local legend maintains that anybody who runs seven times around the Grave will succeed in awakening the giant from his slumbers. Most visitors

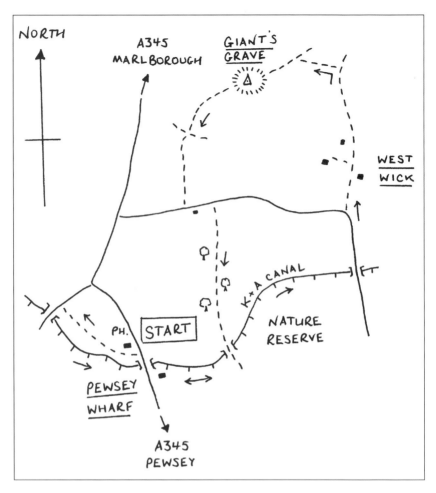

prefer to simply sit and enjoy the views!

Continue down the far side of the hill in the direction of Oare, far below. In the bottom corner of the field, some 400 yards distant, pass through a handgate on the right. The path passes to the right of a small spinney, before crossing the corner of a field to a handgate. This gate brings you onto a track that leads into Oare.

Cross this track, and follow an enclosed path directly opposite. In 75 yards, the path ends by a stile on the left. Cross this stile, turn right and follow the field boundary for $1/4$ mile to Sunnyhill Lane. Turn left and, in just 200 yards, turn right along a bridlepath that continues to the south for $3/4$ mile to Pain's Bridge and the Kennet & Avon Canal. Once

Pewsey Wharf.

over Pain's Bridge, a stile on the right gives access to the towpath which is followed back to Pewsey Wharf and the French Horn.

 KENNET & AVON CANAL – MILKHOUSE WATER BRIDGE TO NEW MILL BRIDGE (¹/₂ MILE)

The towpath follows the south bank of the canal. The downland to the north of the waterway dominates this part of the walk, with Martinsell Hill being a notable landmark.

WOOTTON RIVERS
The Royal Oak
❧

The walk passes through pleasant open countryside before reaching the Kennet & Avon Canal at neighbouring New Mill. Little remains of the former wharf that lay to the west of New Mill Bridge. A 2-mile section of towpath follows, that includes locks 51 to 54 and a selection of overbridges. Beyond lock 54, which gives access to the canal's summit pound, the walk follows quiet lanes and lonely bridlepaths back to Wootton Rivers. The slight elevation enjoyed by these byways brings wide-ranging views across the Wiltshire countryside.

The Royal Oak lies at the northern end of Wootton Rivers' main street, about ¼ mile from the Kennet & Avon Canal. Although not strictly a canalside pub, many a passing barge will moor in the village and its occupants enjoy a short stroll to this most attractive of hostelries. In keeping with the rest of Wootton Rivers, the Royal Oak is a timber-framed building adorned with a magnificent thatched roof.

Internally, there are two main rooms. The L-shaped dining lounge is pleasantly furnished with armchairs, settles and tripod tables. With its low ceilings, beams and woodburning stove, a most cosy atmosphere awaits the inn's customers. The comfortable timbered bar offers patrons the chance to try their hand at a variety of pub games, including darts, pool and chess. On warm summer days, the inn's terrace and beer garden will offer a pleasant alternative for visitors.

The extensive menu at the Royal Oak ranges from basic bar snacks through to dishes that would do justice to many a restaurant. Sandwiches, soups, salads and ploughman's sit alongside more substantial offerings that include local trout, ratatouille with toasted brie topping and lamb with spices, apricot and almonds. If all that were not enough, the range of desserts includes sherry trifle and sticky treacle and almond pudding. To accompany your meal, you could try a glass of scotch – the Royal Oak is well known for its range of whiskies – or a pint of Wadworth 6X or even a Boddingtons. Alternatively, the inn's regular guest beers might prove tempting.

With its idyllic location deep in the Wiltshire countryside, amidst a host of attractive thatched cottages, the Royal Oak is understandably a popular hostelry. At weekends, the pub is often very busy. Telephone: 01672 810322.

● **HOW TO GET THERE:** Leave the A345 Marlborough to Salisbury road at Clench Common, 3 miles south of Marlborough. An unclassified road heads in a south-easterly direction to Wootton Rivers. The Royal Oak lies alongside the T-junction where you turn right into the village's main street.

● **PARKING:** There is a car park for patrons at the Royal Oak, as well as roadside parking in the vicinity of the inn.

● **LENGTH OF THE WALK:** 5 miles. Maps: OS Landrangers 173 Swindon and Devizes and 174 Newbury and Wantage are both needed for this walk (inn GR 197632).

THE WALK

Walk down the main street through Wootton Rivers. The single street through the village is lined with timber-framed and thatch cottages which will soon have you breaking that commandment about 'not coveting thy neighbour's house'! Just off the main street lies St

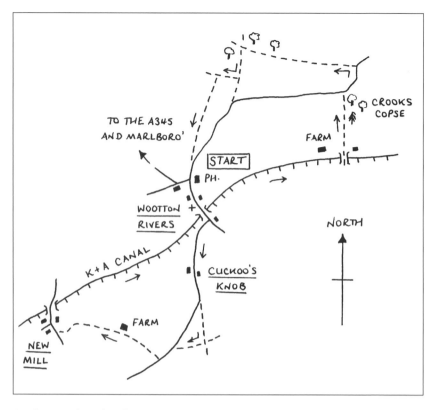

Andrew's church where, as well as repenting of your covetousness, the unusual church clock will certainly catch your eye. Constructed of all manner of junk by a local eccentric, Jack Spratt, its face carries letters rather than numbers. The letters form the text 'TO GOD BE GLORY'.

Cross the Kennet & Avon and the main West of England railway, before turning right along the lane signposted to Milton Lilbourne. In ¼ mile, you will pass through the hamlet of Cuckoo's Knob. At the bottom of a small valley just beyond this settlement, bear left onto an enclosed bridlepath that runs parallel to the road. In 300 yards, at a crosstrack, turn right and you will soon rejoin the Milton Lilbourne road. Turn left and follow the lane for 150 yards to the bottom of a hill, where a footpath on the right is signposted to New Mill.

Follow this footpath across a couple of fields, keeping parallel to – but slightly above – a small stream on your left. Beyond the second field, follow the path across the drive leading to Totteridge Farm, before passing in front of the farmhouse and into open fields. Continue

Lock keeper's cottage, Cadley Lock.

following an ill-defined fieldpath across a couple of fields, the stream still running parallel on the left, until you reach the main West of England railway. Pass through a gap in the fence on the left, and follow a grassy path down to a paddock. Head half-right across this field to a gateway in the far corner, where you join a quiet country lane. Turn right, and follow the lane through the hamlet of New Mill to reach New Mill Bridge and the Kennet & Avon Canal.

 Follow the towpath to the right for 1 mile back to Wootton Rivers, where a left turn will return you to the Royal Oak should you want a shorter walk. For the full walk, continue along the towpath for just over 1 mile. The overbridges around Wootton Rivers were designed as 'carriage bridges' on the instructions of St John's College at Cambridge. The college was a local landowner, and insisted that the bridges be wide enough for carriages and with the minimum of incline on their approaches.

Immediately before Cadley Lock (number 54), cross the overbridge and follow the track/drive northwards for just under ½ mile to a road junction. Turn right, and follow the road uphill for 200 yards to a bridlepath on the left, immediately before the remains of the railway bridge that carried the old Marlborough Railway. Turn left, and follow this bridlepath across the hilltop for ¾ mile to a crossroads.

Turn left at this crossroads, and follow another bridlepath back towards Wootton Rivers. In just 150 yards, pass through a gateway (no gate) on the right into an open field. Follow the left-hand field boundary until, halfway across the field, you cross a stile on the left-hand side. Beyond this stile, follow an enclosed track down Wootton Hill back into Wootton Rivers. Turn right on reaching the road in the village, and you will soon find yourself back at the Royal Oak.

Kʌ KENNET & AVON CANAL

Walks 11 and 12 link up at Cadley Bridge alongside lock 54.

BURBAGE
The Three Horseshoes

*The one-and-a-half miles from Marr Green in the south to Stibb Green in
the north make Burbage arguably the longest village in Wiltshire. For
many years, the main road from Swindon to Salisbury ran through the
heart of Burbage, carrying 6,000 vehicles a day, one in six of which was a
heavy goods vehicle. Fortunately, a bypass has now been constructed
which leaves Burbage an altogether more pleasant place.*

Alongside Stibb Green at the northern end of Burbage is the Three
Horseshoes inn. The pub lies at the end of a terrace of red brick and
thatched properties, although much of the brickwork hereabouts has
been lost beneath a cover of plaster and whitewash. It is a pleasing
setting – cottages, houses and the local pub grouped around a green
– and is certainly all the better for the absence of the heavy traffic
from years gone by.

The Three Horseshoes is one of those pubs that can genuinely be described as being 'olde world'. The front bar – with its beams and inglenook log fire – is what ex-patriates must dream of when reminiscing about traditional English pubs. There is also a second smaller bar, as well as a beer garden which is popular on those warm summer days.

The Three Horseshoes offers a good range of regular pub food, running from sandwiches, ploughman's and soup through to more substantial offerings such as chicken, fish and steak dishes. Being a Wadworth pub, a pint of the flagship 6X brew should be almost obligatory. Brewed in Devizes, the classic beer has been described as 'mid-brown in colour, with a malty and fruity nose and some balancing hop character'. Telephone: 01672 810324.

Note: The Three Horseshoes does not lie on the actual walk, but is just ½ mile to the south of the starting point at the former Savernake Hotel. When the first edition of this book was published, the Savernake Hotel was used as the public house. Following its closure in 1997, the Three Horseshoes in Burbage is the nearest hostelry to the walk. It is advisable to tackle the walk from the former Savernake Hotel, and to drive back to Burbage at the end of the walk.

- **HOW TO GET THERE:** The village of Burbage is now by-passed by the A346 Marlborough to Salisbury Road. To reach the former Savernake Forest Hotel, you will first need to leave the by-pass and drive to the Three Horseshoes inn at the northern end of Burbage. Opposite the inn, follow the minor road signposted to Durley, Savernake and Hungerford. In just ½ mile, you will reach the former Savernake Forest Hotel.
- **PARKING:** Park on the roadside in the vicinity of the former Savernake Forest Hotel.
- **LENGTH OF THE WALK:** 6 miles. Map: OS Landranger 174 Newbury and Wantage (inn GR 235632).

THE WALK

Follow the road northwards from the former Savernake Forest Hotel for ³/₄ mile until, just beyond the hamlet of Durley, you turn left through a gateway to follow a wide grassy ride to the clearly visible Ailesbury Monument. The monument lies ³/₄ mile from the road, just within the confines of Savernake Forest. A classical construction erected by Thomas Bruce, Earl of Ailesbury, the monument stands in memory of

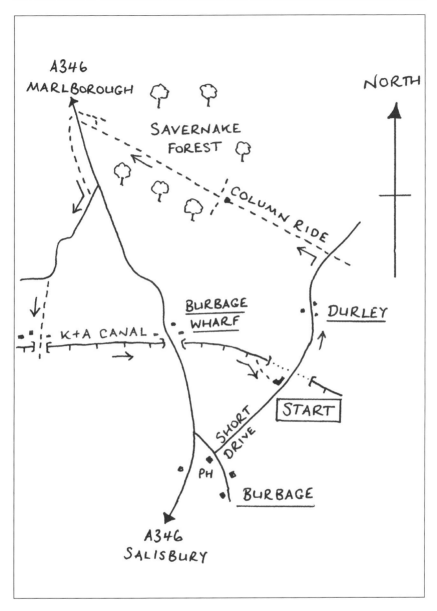

Charles Bruce, a former Earl of Ailesbury, who left the estates hereabouts to his nephew Thomas. Pass the monument, and you reach a prominent forest track – Three Oak Hill Drive. Directly opposite, a single bar wooden gate gives access to another forest track.

Burbage Wharf.

Follow this track westwards for almost 1 mile until, just 100 yards from the clearly visible and audible A346, you turn right along a side track. This brings you to a junction with another forest track in just 100 yards, where you turn left to reach the busy A346.

Cross this main road, and follow the path opposite through the trees. It soon bears to the left, before running parallel to the main road for $^1/_2$ mile to reach a lane leading to Wootton Rivers. Turn right, and follow this lane southwards for just over $^1/_2$ mile to a junction alongside Crooks Copse. At this point, turn left to follow the signposted access drive leading down to Brimslade Farm.

In a little over $^1/_4$ mile, where the lane bears right to the farm, continue ahead to reach the canal by Cadley Lock. Follow the towpath to the left for $1^1/_2$ miles to the western portal of Bruce Tunnel, passing Burbage Wharf along the way.

The Bruce Tunnel is the longest such construction on the whole waterway. The need for a tunnel is perhaps questionable, given that deep cuttings were excavated at either approach to the tunnel which then pierces what is little more than a low hillock. The answer lies in the fact that the Earl of Ailesbury insisted that the tunnel was built to minimise the visual impact that the waterway made upon his estate. The other canal highlight on this section of the walk is Burbage Wharf.

The wharf is the nearest point the canal came to Marlborough, and a steady trade built up in timber, coal, stone and agricultural produce. A splendid crane was erected at the wharf to handle these cargoes. The original crane fell into disrepair some years ago, and was demolished for safety reasons. Today's crane is a replica constructed by a team of soldiers from the REME workshops at Tidworth.

Just before the tunnel, climb some steps on the right, pass beneath the main West of England Railway and follow the footpath beyond for 250 yards back to the road and the former Savernake Forest Hotel.

KENNET & AVON CANAL – THE BRUCE TUNNEL TO WOLFHALL BRIDGE (1 MILE)

The towpath follows the southern bank of the canal. A track opposite the former Savernake Forest Hotel leads down to the eastern end of the tunnel, which is the main feature on this section of the walk.

WILTON
The Swan Inn

Crofton lies at the summit of the Kennet & Avon Canal, marked by the summit reservoir – Wilton Water, and the neighbouring Crofton Pumping Station. Away from the canal, this walk is characterised by far-ranging views across the Wiltshire countryside. Perhaps the most impressive vistas come from the Roman road as it climbs the hillside between Crofton and Wilton.

Although off the beaten track, a lot of visitors seek out the tiny village of Wilton for two major local attractions — a windmill and a pumping station on the Kennet & Avon Canal. The village, with its brick-and-thatch cottages and duck pond, will not disappoint and the Swan, a brick building dating from the turn of the century, will most certainly add to any visitor's enjoyment of a visit to this corner of Wiltshire.

Internally, there is one spacious bar, with a corner reserved for the pool table. Beams, a wood-burning stove, a grandfather clock and a bookcase add elements of interest to the decor, as do a number of prints, photographs of the local fire-brigade in action and a fine selection of brasses. Pine furniture, tables crafted from sewing machine tables, leather-backed chairs and wooden settles complete the furnishings in what happily remains very much a local hostelry.

The menu at the Swan covers the traditional range of dishes – steaks, chicken dishes, fish, ploughman's, jacket potatoes and sandwiches. Amongst the items that caught my eye were chicken tikka masala with rice, ratatouille with grilled brie, beef in black bean sauce with rice, and brunch. This last dish is quite amazing and combines Cumberland sausage, bacon, egg, mushrooms, kidney, potatoes, fried bread, beans and tomatoes! A nice touch on the menu was the simple message requesting patrons to ask for anything that wasn't listed – it could be possible to prepare the dish in question. That will certainly help parents with fussy youngsters!

Real ale enthusiasts will enjoy their visit to the Swan. Amongst the beers available were Wadworth 6X, Hook Norton Best Bitter and Foxley Bitter from nearby Mildenhall. Inches Cider was also on tap. The Swan also offers patrons a good range of wines, the display board listing such delightful tipples as Bordeaux Blanc, Sauvignon, Côtes du Rhone, Corbieres and Minervois.

The Swan has remained a remarkably unspoiled inn over the years. With its sunny garden, its fine village location and the warmth of its welcome, this is one hostelry that you will certainly wish to visit again. Telephone: 01672 870274.

- **HOW TO GET THERE:** Wilton is signposted from the A338 Hungerford road, just 2 miles east of Burbage. The Swan lies in the centre of the village.
- **PARKING:** There is a car park for patrons in front of the Swan. There is also room for careful roadside parking throughout the village.
- **LENGTH OF THE WALK:** $4^1/_2$ miles. Map: OS Landranger 174 Newbury and Wantage (inn GR 268615).

THE WALK

Follow the road outside the Swan, past the pub's garden and on through Wilton. Just past the village duck pond, the road bears left to head towards the edge of Wilton. Turn right onto a track signposted to Freewarren, just before leaving the village. In 250 yards, this track

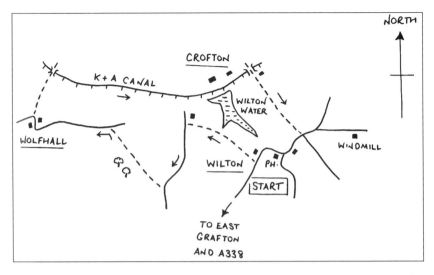

enters an open field. Follow the right-hand hedgerow downhill to the corner of the field, cross a stile and drop down through the trees ahead to a small stream. Cross this stream via a wooden plank, climb the opposite bank and cross a stile into a large open field.

Head directly across this open field until, at the top of the slope, you aim for a stile in the fence ahead. Beyond this stile, cross a small paddock to another stile, where you join Dark Lane. These field paths bring good views of Wilton Water and Crofton Pumping Station. Turn left along the lane and, in 1/2 mile, right onto a footpath signposted to Wolfhall Road. This path leaves the road just before a left-hand bend. The path heads directly uphill across an arable field, following some prominent vehicle tracks. At the far side of the field, continue along this track with a field boundary on your right. The track drops to the bottom of the field where it continues past a small pond up to Wolfhall Road.

Turn left, and follow this quiet lane for 1/2 mile into the hamlet of Wolfhall. After passing Wolfhall Farm, the lane bears left to head towards Burbage. At this point, we continue along the Private Road ahead (footpath only), which reaches the Kennet & Avon Canal in 1/2 mile at Wolfhall Bridge.

Follow the towpath to the right for 1 1/4 miles to reach Wilton Water, Crofton Pumping Station and lock 60. If you cross the canal at lock 60 and bear left, you will find a footpath that passes beneath the main railway line before leading up to the pumping station. The pumps lift water from the reservoir into Crofton Leat, a small channel which

Wilton Water, with Crofton pumping station in the background.

joins the canal over ¹/₂ mile away alongside lock 55. Running alongside the canal at this point are a series of embankments. These mark the course of the Midland & South Western Junction Railway, which ran from Andover through to Cheltenham and crossed the main West of England Railway here. Add another half-a-dozen locks, and it is easy to see why this section of the canal is of great interest to industrial archaeologists.

The pumping station houses a pair of Cornish beam engines, an 1812 Boulton and Watt together with an 1845 Harvey's of Hayle. Both have been carefully restored and returned to full working order, and are believed to be the oldest operational steam engines in the world. The water is drawn from Wilton Water, created artificially by damming a narrow branching valley fed by natural springs. This open stretch of water is a haven for wildfowl, including mallard, heron, coot, moorhen and pochard.

The walk itself continues along to lock 60, where we leave the towpath and follow the enclosed track that climbs the hill on the right. This is the course of an old Roman road which linked Cunetio (Mildenhall, near Marlborough) with Venta Belgarum (Winchester). Wilton Windmill is clearly visible from the Roman road as it reaches the hilltop, with local tradition maintaining that Salisbury Cathedral is also visible on a clear day. Despite its massive 404 foot spire, this latter landmark is in all probability conjecture rather than reality, the product of a drunken imagination!

Continue along the Roman road, as it drops downhill to join the Wilton to Bedwyn road. Turn right, and it is just 5 minutes' walk back to the Swan.

 KENNET & AVON CANAL – LOCK 60 TO BEDWYN CHURCH BRIDGE (2 MILES)

With the towpath keeping to the southern bank of the canal, locks 62 and 63 are features along the way, as is the presence of the main West of England Railway that runs parallel to the canal.

WALK 14

GREAT BEDWYN
The Cross Keys Inn
❦

Between the neighbouring villages of Great Bedwyn and Little Bedwyn, the Kennet & Avon Canal is rapidly approaching the Berkshire border. Rolling downland surrounds the waterway, which runs parallel to the main West of England Railway and the river Dun. This is a delightfully tranquil section of the canal, interrupted only by the occasional lock and the wharf at Great Bedwyn. To the north of the canal lie the historic villages of Chisbury and Great Bedwyn. Between these two villages is Chisbury Wood, an area of mixed woodland that is home to both pheasant and deer.

Great Bedwyn is certainly a village of some status. From the 11th century to the Reform Act of 1832, it was a market town with borough status. Until 1870, a market hall actually stood in the Square. Its site is now marked by an elegant Victorian lamp-post, erected for the Queen's Diamond Jubilee. This part of Great Bedwyn still maintains the look of a small town, with its rows of attractive cottages and its occasional handsome town house.

Overlooking the Square, and just a few minutes walk from the Kennet and Avon Canal, is the Cross Keys Inn. This double-fronted property, with bay windows, was originally of red brick construction, although the brickwork has now been lost beneath a coat of plaster and paintwork. With its hanging baskets and tubs of flowers – and with a fine inn sign depicting a Merlin look-a-like brandishing a pair of keys – the Cross Keys really does add to the village scene.

Internally, the Cross Keys is a spacious old village pub, with comfortable chairs and settles. There are two bar areas, each with ample accommodation for patrons. Being close to the Kennet and Avon Canal, it comes as no surprise to find prints and images around the walls depicting life on this grand waterway. There are also a number of other prints with a waterside theme, illustrating, for example, anglers at play or wildfowl.

The Cross Keys offers a wide choice of reasonably priced food, ranging from ploughman's, soup and filled rolls, through to steak, chicken and fish dishes. There are several good beers available, which might typically include Fuller's London Pride, Greene King Abbott and Courage Best Bitter. It is altogether a most pleasant spot to rest and linger awhile before exploring a fine stretch of the canal. Telephone: 01793 870678.

Note: When the first edition of this book was published, this walk was centred on the Harrow Inn at Little Bedwyn. More recently, the Harrow Inn has become a quite exceptional restaurant with an up-market reputation, and is no longer suitable for inclusion in a book of 'pub walks'. Should you wish to sample the exquisite cuisine at the Harrow, however, simply start the walk at Little Bedwyn. Pre-booking is strongly advised.

● **HOW TO GET THERE:** 4 miles east of Marlborough, on the A4 road to Hungerford, an unclassified road is signposted to Great Bedwyn. In 3 miles, having passed the Three Tuns Inn on the left, you will come to the Square in Great Bedwyn. The Cross Keys lies on the left-hand side, overlooking the Square.

● **PARKING:** Opposite the Cross Keys Inn is Church Street, where there is ample room for roadside parking.

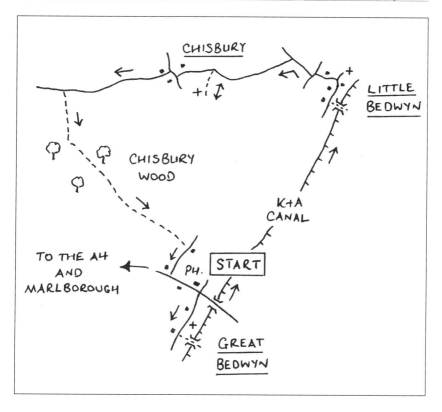

- **LENGTH OF THE WALK:** 5 miles. Map: OS Landranger 174 Newbury and Wantage (inn GR 278646).

THE WALK

Opposite the Cross Keys is Church Street. Head along Church Street, passing a stonemason's museum with displays that include headstones, fonts and fossils. Just past St Mary's church, turn left onto a path signposted to Bedwyn Brail. This path passes alongside the churchyard, before crossing the main West of England railway to reach the Kennet and Avon Canal. Cross the waterway via Bedwyn Church Bridge, and follow the towpath to the left.

Continue along the towpath for 1½ miles to Little Bedwyn. Along the way, you will pass Great Bedwyn Wharf. This was formerly the workplace of a pair of coal merchants who plied the canal, whilst today it provides moorings for a number of pleasure craft, together with a small-scale boat repair service. Walk on past Burnt Mill Lock, Potters

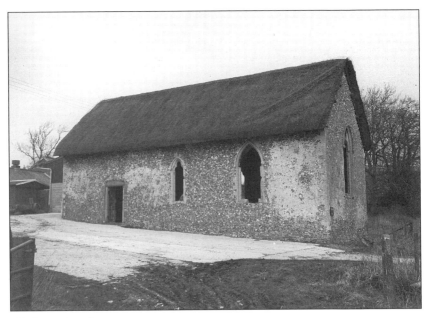

Chisbury chapel.

Lock and Little Bedwyn Lock, with the river Dun being an almost constant companion as the canal follows the bottom of a shallow valley.

Just past Little Bedwyn Lock, cross a footbridge over the main railway line and the canal. At the far side of this bridge, follow the road to the right out of Little Bedwyn, passing the lane leading to the village's Norman church. Continue along the road for 1 mile to the neighbouring village of Chisbury. The views across the Wiltshire countryside will catch your eye on this part of the walk, whilst the signposted path to the derelict 12th-century chapel on the edge of Chisbury should be an obligatory detour. Now owned by English Heritage, it is constructed of local flint and thatch.

At the first junction in Chisbury, turn right. In just a few yards, at a small village green, turn left along the turning signposted to Bedwyn Common. Follow this turning – Chisbury Lane – out of Chisbury. In ¹/₂ mile, a footpath crosses the road. Cross the gateway on the left, following a footpath signposted to Great Bedwyn. This brings you into a large open field. Aim for the far left-hand corner, some 600 yards distant, where a rickety gate leads into Chisbury Wood. Follow the main track ahead, passing Keeper's Cottage on the right-hand side.

In just under ¹/₂ mile, you will reach a prominent crossroads. The main track continues ahead, the right turn drops downhill . . . we follow the left-turn. This track soon bears to the right and continues for 250 yards to a radio mast on the edge of the woodland. The path leaves Chisbury Wood at this point, and follows an uncultivated strip of arable land across a hilltop field and down into Great Bedwyn. This path joins Browns Lane on the edge of Bedwyn. Turn right, and continue to a road junction alongside the Three Tuns in Great Bedwyn. Turn left, and head down to the Square, overlooking which is the Cross Keys Inn.

 KENNET & AVON CANAL – LITTLE BEDWYN LOCK TO FROXFIELD BRIDGE (1¹/₂ MILES)

Locks 68, 69 and 70 are the main canal features on this section of the walk, as the Kennet & Avon passes through lush downland on the Wiltshire/Berkshire border.

WALK 15

HUNGERFORD

The Down Gate

*As the Kennet & Avon approaches Hungerford, the waterway passes
almost imperceptibly from Wiltshire into the Royal County of Berkshire.
Along this section of the canal, the river Dun is a constant companion, a
sparkling tributary of the Kennet which it joins on the edge of Hungerford.
Away from the canal, the walk follows a quiet byway above the Dun valley.
The views are wide and expansive, extending across vast tracts of the
Berkshire and Wiltshire countryside.*

The Down Gate, a whitewashed cottage-style pub, enjoys a delightful
location overlooking the western fringes of Hungerford Common.
Although not a canalside hostelry, the Kennet & Avon is just a few
minutes' walk away across the Common, a pleasant enough stroll for
any passing bargees.

Internally, the Down Gate has two intimate bars, together with a cosy deep-sunk room with an open fire. Wooden tables and chairs, cushioned settles and bar stools form the inn's furnishings, whilst around the bar areas are displayed a number of fascinating collections of artefacts. These include barrel bushes and taps, a collection of miniature spirit bottles, coins, cider pots and blow torches! With a vast collection of tankards hanging from the ceiling beams, and a number of historic photographs of the local area, there is certainly plenty to catch the eye.

A good range of traditional bar food is available at the Down Gate, with the bar menu including fish dishes, butcher's sausages, jacket potatoes, ploughman's, sandwiches, soup, ham, egg and chips and toasted sandwiches. Daily specials are displayed on boards in the bar, and include such tempting options as baguettes, cauliflower cheese, bread and butter pudding and home-made apple pie. The food is well-prepared, reasonably priced and of generous proportions.

The Down Gate is an Arkells pub, part of the Swindon-based brewery founded in 1843. This family-owned concern is run by a great-great-grandson of John Arkell, the founder of the brewery. Arkells 3B and Kingsdown Ale, both available at the Down Gate, are excellent brews, best sampled from the tables in front of the inn overlooking Hungerford Common. A perfect end to a picturesque walk along the Kennet & Avon Canal. Telephone: 01488 682708.

● **HOW TO GET THERE:** Take the A4 to Hungerford, before turning onto the A338 which forms the town's High Street. In a short distance, just beyond the railway bridge over the main street, turn left into Park Street. In $1/4$ mile, the Down Gate lies on the right alongside a cattle grid and the edge of Hungerford Common.

● **PARKING:** Just alongside the pub, there is a large gravelled parking area overlooking Hungerford Common.

● **LENGTH OF THE WALK:** 6 miles. Map: OS Landranger 174 Newbury and Wantage (inn GR 343683).

THE WALK

Follow the road alongside the Down Gate into the centre of Hungerford. Turn right at the High Street and, almost immediately, left into Church Street. Follow Church Street for $1/2$ mile to the edge of the town, before continuing along what becomes a lane that heads out into the Berkshire countryside. The slight elevation of this byway

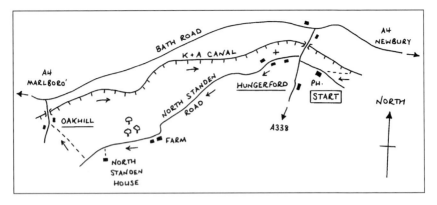

brings open views to the north across the Dun valley. In $3/4$ mile, you pass North Standen Farm and, in less than $1/2$ mile, the entrance to North Standen House. Just 250 yards up the lane past the driveway leading to North Standen House, turn right along a bridleway signposted to Oakhill.

Follow this bridleway across open hilltop fields, before dropping downhill into the diminutive hamlet of Oakhill. Turn right at the road and, in just 100 yards, you will reach the Kennet & Avon Canal at Froxfield Bridge.

Follow the towpath to the right back into Hungerford. Along the way, you will pass locks 71 to 74 before reaching Hungerford Wharf, with the river Dun running parallel for much of the route. Hungerford Wharf saw its first cargo – Russian tallow — arrive in 1798 from Newbury. This was the limit of the Kennet Navigation that linked the town with the Thames. Although the wharf's crane and gauging station are now little more than a fading memory, the original wharfside buildings remain, albeit converted to residential use. Just before Cobbler's Lock – number 72 – it is worth crossing a stile on the right to view the tiny, three-arched Dun Aqueduct. Also, look out for the footbridge that literally crosses the lock chamber at lock 73, Freeman's Marsh Lock, a unique sight on the British canal network.

Back in Hungerford, the towpath passes alongside St Lawrence's church. The church is virtually unrecognisable from that seen in early prints. Gone are the fascinating blend of angles, destroyed when the weight of heavy snow caused the roof to collapse in 1814. In their place is a substantial tonnage of Bath stone, one of the earliest cargoes carried along the Kennet & Avon to the town.

Continue along the towpath beyond the wharf, initially passing

Hungerford Wharf.

beneath Hungerford's High Street. In ½ mile, cross a stile in the fence on the right, pass beneath the railway and climb onto Hungerford Common. Bear half-right across the Common, and in 200 yards you will reach the Down Gate.

 KENNET & AVON CANAL – HUNGERFORD COMMON TO DUNMILL LOCK BRIDGE (½ MILE)

Along this section of the walk, the canal is bounded by the river Kennet to the north and Hungerford Common to the south.

WALK 16

KINTBURY
The Blue Ball

❧

This walk begins by following the quiet lanes and byways to the south of the Kennet & Avon Canal. Foxley Covert, an area of mixed woodland, and Hungerford Common are particular highlights on this section of the walk. Dun Mill, just north of where the walk joins the canal, marks the confluence of the Dun with the Kennet, whose water meadows parallel the canal on the return leg back to Kintbury.

Kintbury was traditionally an agricultural community, a village set in the fertile Berkshire countryside. In 1830, a group of local farm labourers concerned at increasing mechanisation on their farms organised themselves into a collection of rural Luddites. Ricks were set alight, riots were commonplace and items of farm machinery were smashed. The group's headquarters was the Blue Ball pub, where one meeting was rudely interrupted by a detachment of Grenadier Guards summoned from London. One hundred arrests were made, with the majority of labourers being transported to Australia or imprisoned. The most unfortunate member of the group was one John Winterbourne, who was hanged at Reading Gaol.

Today, the Blue Ball is an altogether more peaceful hostelry, with the only source of conflict taking place on the pool table in the public bar! The inn is a bright, whitewashed building, fronting onto Kintbury's High Street 500 yards south of Kintbury Bridge and the Kennet & Avon Canal. Internally, there are three interconnected rooms – a public bar, a lounge bar and a dining area. Low ceilings, the occasional beam, exposed brickwork and open fireplaces lend the inn a traditional atmosphere. This is complemented by wooden settles, prints, copper artefacts and horse brasses.

A good range of traditional pub fare is available at the Blue Ball, with the menu covering fish and vegetarian dishes, filled jacket potatoes, sandwiches, ploughman's, salads and children's dishes. Vegetarians might be tempted by mushroom Stroganoff, potato and leek pie or broccoli cheese, whilst youngsters can choose from a number of trusty favourites including burgers, chicken nuggets, fish fingers and sausages. The food is well prepared and represents good value-for-money.

A number of fine beers are available at the Blue Ball, including Wadworth 6X, Courage Best and Morlands Old Speckled Hen. If you prefer to quench your thirst in the open air, there is a pleasant beer garden at the rear of the pub. A friendly and relaxing hostelry, that will provide welcome sustenance at the end of a pleasant walk through the Berkshire countryside. Telephone: 01488 608126.

● **HOW TO GET THERE:** Leave the A4 just 3 miles east of Hungerford, and follow an unclassified road heading south into Kintbury. As you enter the village, Station Road crosses the Kennet & Avon Canal before leading up to the High Street. You will find the Blue Ball 100 yards along the High Street on the right-hand side.

● **PARKING:** There is a car park for patrons alongside the Blue Ball. There is also room for roadside parking on the High Street outside the pub.

● **LENGTH OF THE WALK:** $5\frac{1}{2}$ miles. Map: OS Landranger 174 Newbury and Wantage (inn GR 382669).

THE WALK

Follow the High Street on out of Kintbury for 400 yards to a junction.

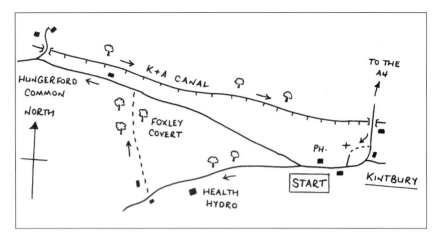

Fork left along a quiet lane signposted to Inglewood Health Hydro. In little more than 1 mile, having passed the impressive building housing the Health Hydro, turn right along a metalled lane. This is just before Templeton Stud. Follow this lane – it is officially a bridlepath – for 3/4 mile to its junction with the Hungerford Road, passing through Foxley Covert along the way.

Turn left and follow the Hungerford Road for 3/4 mile to a right-turn signposted to Lower Denford. Although the Hungerford Road carries a fair few cars, it is not long before it crosses a cattle grid to enter Hungerford Common, where you can walk on the grass alongside the road. Take the Lower Denford turning, which crosses the main West of England Railway before reaching the Kennet & Avon Canal at Dunmill Lock Bridge.

Follow the towpath to the right, passing three more locks (Wire, Brunsden's and Kintbury), for just over 2 miles back into Kintbury, the towpath running parallel to the Kennet's water meadows for much of the way. Leave the towpath at Kintbury Wharf. The wharf can claim a spot in Kennet & Avon Canal history, being the destination of the first official barge along the waterway. On 12th June 1797, a 60-ton barge carrying the band of the 15th Regiment of Dragoons, made the 6-mile trip from Newbury to Kintbury in 2½ hours. Subsequently, the wharf saw cargo of a more commercial nature coming its way – iron and coke from South Wales to be used in local ironworks manufacturing agricultural equipment. Whiting – a fine powder made from the local chalk and used in paint manufacturing – was an important cargo shipped from Kintbury to Bristol's paint manufacturers.

Follow Station Road to the right back into Kintbury. In 100 yards, follow a footpath on the right which brings you to a lane beside St Mary's church. Charles Dundas, the first chairman of the Kennet & Avon Canal Company, became lord of the local manor in the late 18th century and there is a monument to him in the church, whose 12th-century origins have largely been lost due to much Victorian 'improvement'. Follow the path through the churchyard, turning left by the church porch, to rejoin the lane which leads down to the High Street. A right-turn will return you to the Blue Ball.

 KENNET & AVON CANAL – KINTBURY WHARF TO HAMSTEAD BRIDGE (2¹/₂ MILES)

With the towpath following the north bank of the canal, locks 79 and 80 are passed along the way, with the canal lying in the shadows of Irish Hill to the south. The river Kennet is an ever-present companion along this leg of the walk, and actually becomes the waterway between lock 80 and Hamstead Bridge.

WALK 17

MARSH BENHAM
The Red House

A gentle excursion deep in the Kennet valley, that follows a short section of the Kennet & Avon's towpath between Hamstead Lock and Benham Lock. Woodland, natural and man-made watercourses, the locks and their accompanying bridges all combine to produce a delightful rural landscape. Benham Broad is the highlight along this section of the canal, a beautiful spot where the river Kennet flows in and out of the navigation to form a wide expanse of water akin to Wilcot Wide Water further west.

The Red House at Marsh Benham is an attractive brick-and-thatch hostelry, lying just above the river Kennet and its water meadows. The inn may lie off the beaten track, but that has not prevented many customers discovering its charm, its cuisine and its fine beers, making it one of the more popular hostelries in the area.

Previously known as 'The Water Rat', this inn has been totally refurbished in recent years, with a new kitchen and dining room having been added to complement the large and inviting bar area. Many visitors prefer to relax in the inn's attractive gardens, especially on the lawns that slope away towards the water meadows and the river.

The choice of dishes is both diverse and imaginative, focusing on simple but good food. Customers can enjoy a quick light plate of food or alternatively a full sit-down lunch or dinner. The menu also includes daily specials, offering local fish and game. The Red House uses only fresh and high quality ingredients, and can boast an award-winning chef in its kitchens.

After a pleasant stroll in the Berkshire countryside, you can rest assured that a range of real ales will be available at the Red House. The brews could include Shepherd Neame Spitfire, Theakston XB or Wadworth 6X. Excellent food, fine beers and a friendly hostelry, the perfect combination. Telephone: 01635 582017.

- **HOW TO GET THERE:** Just 2 miles west of Newbury, the turning to Marsh Benham heads off south from the A4. In $1/2$ mile, the Red House lies on the left by a minor crossroads.
- **PARKING:** There are car parks alongside the Red House for customers, as well as some roadside parking in the vicinity of the inn. If you prefer, to avoid repeating a section of road walking at the start/finish of the walk, there is limited roadside parking by the canal, 400 yards south of the Red House (see map).
- **LENGTH OF THE WALK:** 3 miles. Map: OS Landranger 174 Newbury and Wantage (inn GR 426675).

THE WALK

At the crossroads just along from the Red House, turn left and follow the road for 400 yards down to the Kennet & Avon at Hamstead Bridge, crossing the main West of England Railway at a level crossing shortly before the canal.

Follow the towpath to the left for $1^1/_4$ miles as far as Benham Lock, passing Benham Broad en route. Leave the towpath at this point, and follow the track across the overbridge into an open field. Cross to a stile/gate at the far side of this field, beyond which you follow an enclosed track up through Enborne Copse to the Newbury to Enborne road.

Turn right, and follow the road for nearly $1/2$ mile until you come to

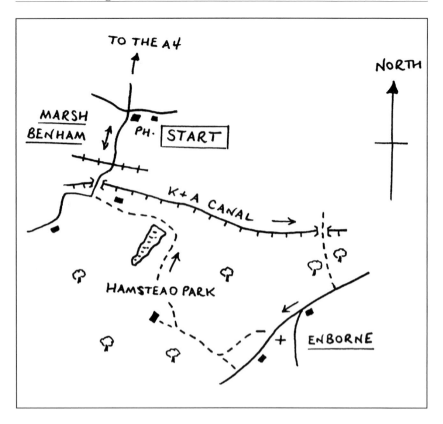

Enborne church on the left and the entrance to Hamstead Park on the right. Turn right, and follow the driveway leading to Hamstead House. The drive passes through the attractive landscaped grounds towards the house. The magnificent grounds of Hamstead Park, a 700-acre estate, were visited by royalty as far back as the 15th century. Richard III enjoyed visits to the hunting lodge and noted the fine sport in his correspondence. From 1620 until 1984, the estate was in the hands of the Craven family but death duties led to its sale in 1984.

Two hundred yards from the house, the signposted path leaves the drive and bears half-right to reach the corner of the hedge surrounding Hamstead House. Continue following the far side of the hedgerow downhill to a handgate, beyond which the path climbs a gentle slope to rejoin a drive leading away from Hamstead House.

Follow this driveway to the right, ignoring one early right-turn. The drive winds its way downhill to cross the ornamental lake in Hamstead

Park, before joining the road in Marsh Benham just to the south of the river Kennet and the canal. Follow the road to the right for 400 yards, and you will return to that minor crossroads alongside the Red House.

 **KENNET & AVON CANAL – BENHAM LOCK TO WOOLHAMPTON BRIDGE (9 MILES)**

The towpath switches banks no fewer than six times along the way! No pub walk has been included in this area due to the presence of Greenham Common airfield, Newbury racecourse and industrial sites at Colthrop and Thatcham, which block any realistic circular walks. Eleven locks lie along this section of the canal, as well as the unique turf-sided lock at Monkey Marsh. There is also the town of Newbury to explore, whose waterside has been described as a 'delightful interlude'. The Town Bridge in Newbury is the official link between the old Kennet Navigation and the more recent Kennet & Avon Canal.

WOOLHAMPTON
The Rowbarge

The Kennet Navigation between Newbury and Reading received the Royal Assent in 1715 and the mixture of artificial cut and navigable river was completed some nine years later under the watchful eye of its chief engineer, John Hore. This walk explores a section of the Navigation, running between Woolhampton and Aldermaston Wharf. This is perhaps the most delightful river section along the length of the Kennet & Avon, with the river winding its timeless course through water meadows and woodland.

The Rowbarge enjoys an idyllic location alongside lock 94 and the navigable Kennet in Woolhampton. In 1940 Tom and Angela Rolt were cruising the waterway in their vessel *Cressy* when they encountered the somewhat decrepit Woolhampton Swingbridge. Their log records:

'With half the able-bodied males of the village heaving on crow-bars under the direction of the red-faced landlord of the 'Row Barge' and with *Cressy* going full astern, her bow line fast to a bridge railing post, it took us three hours to open the bridge at Woolhampton.'

Today's landlord enjoys a more restful occupation than his predecessor and is host at a delightful white-washed hostelry, ablaze with tubs of flowers and hanging baskets in summer months. To the side of the inn is a large garden with lawns running down to the Kennet, overlooked by the Rowbarge's conservatory. Internally, the Rowbarge consists of a traditional beamed bar, an adjoining panelled room and a small snug. The various artefacts that adorn the bar areas include a selection of cricketing mementoes as well as a vast collection of brass blowlamps.

The Rowbarge has built up a well-deserved reputation for the quality of its food. The dishes range from filled jacket potatoes and filled French bread, through to home-made pies, vegetable bake and tagliatelle carbonara. A fine range of beers is available to accompany your meal. The choice includes Brakspear SB, Fuller's London Pride and Greene King Abbot. A picturesque inn, an idyllic location and a relaxing walk in the Kennet valley, the ingredients of a perfect day out. Telephone: 0118 971 2213.

- **HOW TO GET THERE:** Woolhampton lies on the A4 between Newbury and Theale. In the centre of the village, turn into Station Road – signposted to the station! The Rowbarge lies 200 yards past the railway level crossing, on the right-hand side, immediately past the river Kennet.
- **PARKING:** There is a car park for patrons alongside the Rowbarge. A number of parking spaces are also available for visitors to the canal.
- **LENGTH OF THE WALK:** 5 miles. Maps: OS Landrangers 174 Newbury and 175 Reading (inn GR 573665).

THE WALK

Retrace your steps back to the river Kennet and Woolhampton Bridge, and follow the towpath to the right for 1/2 mile to a wooden footbridge – number 18. This is a new construction that replaced the former Wickham Knight Swingbridge. Cross the Kennet, and continue following the towpath along the opposite bank of the river. In 1/4 mile, the river bears off to the right, whilst the towpath

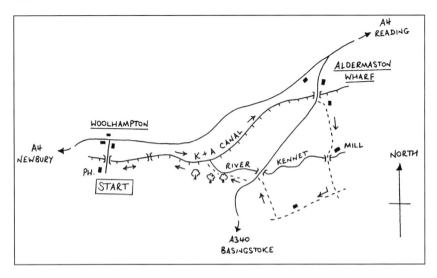

continues alongside Salmon Cut, an artificial section of waterway. Follow the Cut for 1¼ miles to Aldermaston Wharf and the A340, the towpath changing banks at Froudes Bridge along the way.

The original Aldermaston Wharf lay to the east of the swingbridge carrying the A340 over the Kennet & Avon. In 1852, when the GWR assumed control of the canal, a second wharf was created to connect with the railway west of the road bridge. The new wharf lies alongside Aldermaston Lock, originally one of the turf-sided locks unique to the Kennet & Avon Canal. The turf has long gone, but has been replaced with magnificent scalloped brickwork.

Leave the towpath at Aldermaston Wharf, cross the A340 and follow the gravelled road opposite the short distance to Bridge House. Turn right in front of Bridge House, and follow Mill Lane, an unmetalled road. In ½ mile, at the end of a section of wooden fencing on the right, turn right onto an enclosed footpath. Follow this path down to the Kennet and an associated series of millstreams. Cross the various waterways using a series of footbridges, and continue to a stile and an open field. Head directly across the field ahead for 30 yards, before crossing a watercourse on a wooden footbridge. Once across the stream, turn sharp right to follow this watercourse across two fields. In the corner of the second field, pass through a gateway to join an unmetalled road.

Continue along this track for close on ½ mile until, 250 yards beyond Fisherman's Cottage, a public footpath is signposted on the right leading into open fields. Head directly across the first field to a shallow valley on the far side. In this dip, cross a footbridge and a stile into a second field. Continue directly across this field, before crossing another footbridge and a stile into a third field. Head across this field towards a copse of poplars. Just a few yards up from the left-hand corner of this copse, cross a footbridge and follow a path through the trees until you reach the A340. Turn left, and follow the busy A340 with care for 200 yards, to a footpath signposted on the right.

Leave the main road, and follow this path – it shortly crosses a footbridge to enter a field on the right-hand side. Follow the left-hand edge of this field to another wooden footbridge across a stream. In the next field, follow the well-worn path directly ahead that winds its way up to the banks of the Kennet. Follow the path alongside the river until you reach the point where Salmon Cut joins the river. At this point, follow a footpath through an area of woodland for 200 yards before rejoining the riverbank. This path effectively cuts off a small loop in the river. Continue following the riverbank – this is now the navigable Kennet – back to bridge number 18. Retrace your steps back along the towpath to the Rowbarge.

 KENNET & AVON CANAL

Walks 18 and 19 connect at Aldermaston Wharf.

ALDERMASTON WHARF
The Butt Inn

Features of interest on this walk include the Visitors Centre at Aldermaston Wharf, the wharf itself, three locks and a collection of swing bridges that regularly delay traffic on the lanes leading south from the A4. South of the waterway, the walk passes through low-lying meadow and wetland bordering the Kennet and its various tributaries. The final section of riverside path leading to Padworth Mill is especially enjoyable, being a haven for wildfowl.

Despite being the main transhipment area between Reading and Newbury, there was never a waterside hostelry at Aldermaston Wharf. This is all the more surprising given that a local family by the name of Strange once ran a brewery alongside Aldermaston Lock, earning the lock the nickname of 'Brewhouse' at one time. Thirsty bargees had to head south along the main road running through Aldermaston Wharf to find a glass of beer; 200 yards south of the waterway, they would have found the Butt Inn.

Butt translates as 'target' or 'shooting range', which explains the inn's somewhat odd-looking sign displaying a target complete with protruding arrow heads! Whether this was the site of shooting competitions in years past can be but a matter of speculation. The sign adorns a red-brick building fronting onto the main A340 road heading south towards Basingstoke.

Internally, the Butt Inn is an unpretentious local hostelry. To the right as you enter the inn is the public bar, whilst to the left lie a series of interconnecting rooms housing the lounge bar, a pool room and a dining area. Reproduction furniture sets provide ample seating for customers, with open fireplaces providing warmth in mid-winter. Around the walls are displayed prints of birds and wildfowl, whilst alongside the bar are a series of photographs of fish that failed to escape the anglers on the nearby Kennet. On warm summer days, customers can relax in the garden to enjoy their food and drink.

The Butt Inn offers all those old favourites associated with traditional pub fare, including burgers, ploughman's, chicken, steak and fish dishes. More unusual offerings which might tempt your palate include beef vindaloo, chicken korma, ratatouille bake, swordfish steaks and pork in cider. To accompany your meal, beers such as Boddingtons and Flowers are available, as well as the house ale – Butts Bitter. Butts Bitter at the Butt Inn, the ideal way to end a delightful walk through the Kennet valley. Telephone: 0118 971 2129.

- **HOW TO GET THERE:** 8 miles east of Newbury, leave the main A4 to follow the A340 into Aldermaston Wharf. The A340 crosses the Kennet & Avon Canal in just $1/4$ mile, and in another 200 yards you will find the Butt Inn on the right-hand side.
- **PARKING:** There is a car park for patrons opposite the Butt Inn. Back in Aldermaston Wharf, there is a car park by the clearly signposted Canal Centre, which lies alongside the towpath at the start of this walk.
- **LENGTH OF THE WALK:** 5 miles. Map: OS Landranger 175 Reading and Windsor (inn GR 601670).

THE WALK

From the Butt Inn, walk back up the A340 to the Kennet & Avon. Follow the towpath to the right, signposted to Padworth Bridge. The path initially passes the whitewashed Visitors Centre and

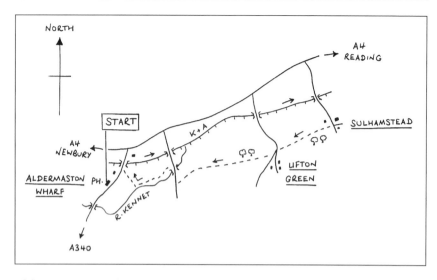

Aldermaston Wharf, before reaching Padworth Lock. The Centre was originally a canalman's cottage, constructed at the turn of the 19th century; today, it serves as a tea-room, bookshop and information centre. After the lock, continue along the towpath for another 400 yards to Padworth Swingbridge.

Continue along the towpath for 1 mile to Ufton Swingbridge, passing Towney Lock along the way. The towpath changes banks at Ufton Bridge. Cross the canal and the adjoining Kennet, before turning left to continue along the riverbank. The Kennet now forms the navigation. Follow the river for 3/4 mile to Tyle Mill Swingbridge and the neighbouring lock. To the south of the navigation is low-lying meadowland, managed by the Countryside Commission to maintain its traditional qualities.

Leave the navigation at Tyle Mill Swingbridge, and follow the road to the right into Sulhamstead. Immediately past Rose Court, the first house on the right in the village, turn right onto an enclosed footpath that crosses a couple of stiles before reaching an open field. Follow the right-hand side of this field to a stile which gives access to a newly planted hillside plantation. Head directly across this plantation to another stile, and in the next field cross to a gateway. In the next field, continue walking in the same direction with the field boundary on your right. Towards the far side of this hillside pasture, the path heads up to the top left-hand corner of the field and yet another stile. Continue alongside the left-hand field boundaries of two further small fields, to a stile which brings you onto the lane leading into Ufton Green.

Cross the road and the green opposite, and follow the lane signposted to Ufton Court. In just 150 yards, cross a stile on the right to follow a signposted footpath. Follow the fence on the right for 15 yards and, where it ends, continue directly ahead across a large open pasture to a stile almost in the far corner. Follow the right-hand field boundary in the next field to a stile, just a few yards up from the bottom corner of the field. Cross a broken stile, and continue along a well-defined path that runs alongside an area of woodland. At the far side of this field, turn right along a farm track. Shortly, the path bears left to run along the bottom of the field to reach a gateway. Continue directly ahead across the middle of the next two fields to reach an enclosed track. Follow this track for ¼ mile down to the lane leading into Padworth.

Turn right, and follow the lane across a tributary of the Kennet before crossing the Kennet itself. Immediately past the river, descend some steps on the left to join the riverbank. Follow the riverbank for almost ½ mile, until bushes and trees surrounding Padworth Mill mark the end of the riverside right-of-way. During springtime, Canada geese and mute swans congregate along this part of the river with their young offspring. Do not approach the proud parents, however. Swans become very possessive and aggressive at this time of year! At this point, cross a stile and follow a path through an area of woodland to Mill Lane. Turn right, and follow Mill Lane for ½ mile back to the A340. A left-turn will bring you back to the Butt Inn.

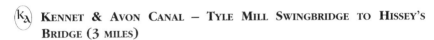

KENNET & AVON CANAL – TYLE MILL SWINGBRIDGE TO HISSEY'S BRIDGE (3 MILES)

The towpath follows the southern bank of the waterway throughout. The canal borders an area of reclaimed gravel pits on this section of the walk, whose waters are now used for a variety of leisure pursuits. Along the waterway, your steps will pass locks 100 to 102, as well as one of the ugliest bridges along the waterway – the cold, grey construction that carries the M4!

BURGHFIELD BRIDGE
The Cunning Man
❦

*B*etween *Theale and Reading, the canal passes through an increasingly urbanised landscape, with the imprints of development on every side. This short walk explores a green oasis around Burghfield, consisting of a reed-lined section of the canal, the waters of the Kennet and reclaimed gravel pits. Along the Kennet & Avon you will pass Hissey's Bridge, Burghfield Lock and Cut, Southcote Lock and the delightfully named Milkmaid's Footbridge.*

The Cunning Man is a red-brick hostelry, whose garden backs onto the Kennet & Avon. The inn sign depicts the gentleman in question, a game hunter, off in pursuit of prey with his shotgun and bullets. Presumably, his quest would have taken him along the riverbank of the nearby Kennet, where he would have engaged in a spot of fly-fishing to add variety to his diet. This theme is continued inside the Cunning Man, with a number of fishing prints together with a display case of fly-fishing artefacts.

The Cunning Man, now a part of the Harvester chain, has been the subject of extensive renovation in recent years. Whilst the focus of the Harvester group is on the restaurants, there is still a 'pub' area at the Cunning Man. This long bar area is carpeted throughout, and is furnished with reproduction darkwood table and chair sets, together with the occasional cushioned settle. A brick fireplace and print wallpaper complete the comfortable decor. As well as the fishing prints and artefacts, maps of the canal and old photographs of the waterway and scenes on the Thames are displayed around the walls.

There is a separate pub menu for visitors not using the restaurant. The dishes available include soup, filled jacket potatoes, various basket meals and sandwiches. The basket meals include hickory smoked chicken wings, spiced beanburgers, scampi and bangers, all served basket-style with fries and dipping pots. The farmhouse style, soft-grain sandwiches are served with coleslaw and fries, with fillings including maple smoked ham, tuna, prawns and ham 'n' cheese. If your appetite permits, there is also a dessert menu that includes hot chocolate fudge cake, apple and blueberry crumble and ice cream sundae.

A range of beers is available at the Cunning Man, that includes Bass, Caffreys and Worthington Bitter. Between the inn and the canal is a large garden, with extensive lawns and myriad picnic tables. This is a cool shady spot, ideal for enjoying a refreshing pint after a short stroll along the adjoining waterway. Telephone: 0118 959 0771.

- **HOW TO GET THERE:** Follow the A4 from Theale towards Reading and 2 miles on from junction 12 on the M4 motorway – the Theale junction – you pass the George and Dragon pub. At the traffic lights just past the pub, follow the turning signposted to Burghfield. In 1 mile, you cross the Kennet & Avon and the Cunning Man lies on the right-hand side of the road.
- **PARKING:** There is a large car park for patrons alongside the Cunning Man. Alternatively, there is room for careful roadside parking in Mill Road just south of the inn.
- **LENGTH OF THE WALK:** 5 miles. Map: OS Landranger 175 Reading and Windsor (inn GR 680707).

THE WALK

(N.B. The first $1^1/_2$ miles of the walk to Hissey's Bridge includes a lakeside path that runs within 25 yards of the M4. A shorter walk,

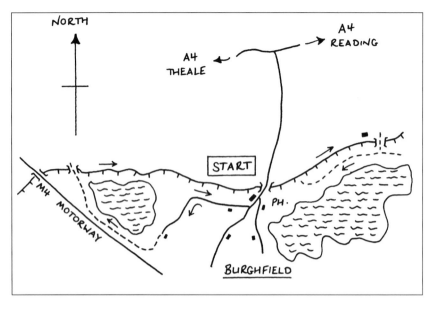

missing out this part can be enjoyed by starting at ***.)

Return from the pub to the main road, turn right for 150 yards before turning right into Mill Road. Follow Mill Road for 3/4 mile, until it ends by a private road that gives access to a cottage. This section of roadwalking passes several flooded gravel pits along the way.

Turn right along the gravelled track giving access to Theale Water Ski Club. The track bears left, before following the edge of a flooded gravel pit for 3/4 mile to a parking area immediately south of the Kennet & Avon. This section of the walk is unfortunately totally dominated by the roar of traffic on the adjoining M4 motorway, but this will be left behind on joining the canal towpath.

Pass through the car park, cross Hissey's Bridge and follow the navigable Kennet to the right for 1 mile to Swan's Roving Footbridge. Along the way, you will enter the Burghfield Cut as well as passing Burghfield Lock. Cross the canal and follow the towpath for 1/4 mile to the Cunning Man. (***) Continue along the towpath for 1 mile to Southcote Lock and Milkmaid's Footbridge. At one point on this section of the canal, the river Kennet winds its way in and out, forming excellent natural moorings.

Just past Southcote Lock, cross a footbridge on the right over the river Kennet. Follow the footpath to the right, past a millpool and a pond. The path then winds its way through an area of bushes and trees

Hissey's Bridge.

for 150 yards before joining the south bank of the Kennet. Follow the riverbank for just under ¹/₂ mile back to the canal, ignoring a left-turn at a junction just before the towpath. It is however worth turning off to the left along this riverbank path to follow cul-de-sac tracks that lead down to the flooded gravel pits. Back on the towpath, turn left and retrace your steps to the Cunning Man.

 KENNET & AVON CANAL – SOUTHCOTE LOCK TO THAMES MOUTH IN READING (4 MILES)

Along this increasingly urbanised section of the canal, you will pass Southcote Pumping Station, County Lock and Blake's Lock, as well as the surviving remnants of various wharves and warehouses.

Kennet & Avon Canal Information and Accommodation

Tourist Information Centres

Bath – Abbey Chambers, Abbey Churchyard, Bath BA1 1LY.
Tel: (01125) 477101.
Bradford-on-Avon – 34 Silver Street, Bradford-on-Avon, BA15 3JX.
Tel: (01125) 865797.
Trowbridge – St Stephen's Place, Trowbridge, BA14 8AH.
Tel: (01225) 777054.
Melksham – Church Street, Melksham, SN12 6LS. Tel: (01225) 707424.
Devizes – 39 St John's Street, Devizes, SN10 1BN. Tel: (01125) 729408.
Avebury – The Great Barn, Avebury, SN8 1RF. Tel: (01672) 539425.
Marlborough – Car Park, George Lane, SN8 1EE. Tel: (01672) 513989.
Newbury – The Wharf, Newbury, RG14 5AS. Tel: (01635) 519431.
Reading – The Town Hall, Blagrave Street, RG1 1QH.
Tel: 0118 956 6226.

Accommodation

There is an abundance of accommodation all the way along the Kennet & Avon Canal. The Southern Tourist Board in conjunction with British Waterways have published a booklet entitled *The Kennet & Avon Canal Accommodation Guide* which is available from any of the above TICs.

The booklet provides details of 25 establishments offering accommodation, including charges and descriptions of each property.